Reliance Motor

Of Newbury — A Centenary Album

Written and published by Paul Lacey

Philip Wallis caught this selection of the fleet during the heyday of operations, with Duple (Midland)-bodied Bedford SBO service saloon No.80 (SX 8901). Bedford SBO coach No.71 (219 BRE), Bedford coach No.94 (OEL 933) with Duple 'Super Vega' coachwork of 1954, plus one of the very stylish Burlingham 'Seagull'-bodied AEC 'Reliance' centre-entrance coaches No.46 (MJB 820) in use from 1956 to 1973, all parked at the Boundary Road Garage. The mix of Bedford and AECs was the mainstay of operations for several decades, along with lesser numbers of Leyland and other types, the double-deckers becoming necessary for some of the contract operations.

Written, designed, typeset and published by Paul Lacey

17 Sparrow Close, Woosehill,

Wokingham, Berkshire, RG41 3HT

ISBN 978-0-9567832-9-5

Printed by Biddles Books, King's Lynn, Norfolk, PE32 1SF

CONTENTS

ACKNOWLEDGEMENTS

A work of this nature, researched on-and-off over 50 years alongside other projects, has involved input from many sources, so my apologies are tendered should any go without acknowledgement here. Generally, I have spent much time perusing the local newspapers of the time, so thanks to the Library Staff in Newbury and Reading, along with the Berkshire Archives. I am also grateful to my fellow researchers for making available information they had gleaned, as well as my contacts at the Omnibus Society and PSV Circle. Much personal information was also taken from the Census, work I undertook often parallel to my own Family History activities.

However, such a history would be largely unrecorded had it not been for the personal contributions of those who were there at the time, and indeed those active in such operations. In that respect, much very interesting material was provided during interviews with members and employees of those involved with Newbury & District and Reliance, and with the Austin and Hedges families, as 2022 marks the centenary of the inception of Reliance Motor Services.

I am also appreciative of the photographers, both past and present, who have kindly made available their prints to use in this book, in particular Brian Botley, David Gillard, Mac Head, Ted Jones, Thomas W.W. Knowles, Graham Low, Bob Mack, Martin Shaw, Ray Simpson, Philip Wallis and Paul White, along with the historic collections now part of The Bus Archive in Walsall, plus the assistance with appeals from the Newbury Weekly News and use of its Archive, as 2022 marks the centenary of the inception of Reliance Motor Services.

Also, published in 2020 was the excellent Pen & Sword book entitled Reliance Motor Services – The Story of a Family-owned Independent Bus Company, co-written by family member Barrie Hedges and local transport enthusiast David Wilder which, as the title suggests is very much from the family perspective, and based on the day-to-day life of Reliance from its formation to the final sale, which is recommended reading. My volume The Newbury & District Motor Services Story, provides a fuller perspective on all other local transport developments throughout the decades from the 1900's to the 1950's, also well worth a read, still available direct from the author - see page 64 for details.

However, it is the intention that this album will compliment both of those, to provide a fuller understanding of the role of contract operations, along with   illustrations of the fleet as it developed over the six decades when they were a daily site throughout West Berkshire and many places beyond.   **Paul Lacey, Wokingham January 2022**

The inclusion of double-deckers always made for additional interest when visiting Reliance, though much of their work went on unseen, as primarily for contract operations to AERE Harwell and AWRE Aldermaston, but sometimes also appeared on the public routes. As such, they hailed from far and wide, so Graham Low caught this interesting pair in the Mill Lane yard, with former Newcastle CT AEC 'Regent' No.52 (JVK 633) and former Ribble double-deck coach No.78 (DCK 219) on Leyland 'Titan' chassis, one of the original batch of 'White Lady' express vehicles.

RX 6888 was an original George Hedges vehicle, which passed with his business into *N&D* in September 1932, on a Ford AA-type chassis with a 14-seater 'sunshine coach' body by Duple. It is seen here with driver George Amor, who worked for various local operators, but it returned to the Hedges ownership in 1934 and ran until sold in 1942 to be used as a lorry. It is not recorded as having a fleet number when with Reliance.

No.7 (AKE 393) was a Commer 'Centaur' new to *Auto Pilots* based in Folkestone, shown on its express route into London, carrying a 20-seater Duple coach body and new in 1932, coming to Brightwalton by 1937 after the original owner had sold out to *East Kent*. This photo was by pioneer enthusiast Joe Higham, but how long it sremained with Reliance is not certain, or if had any further owners.

No.10 (MW 2985) is shown here partly to represent similar GMC **No**.**3. (SH 3380),** with its 6-cylinder American-design engine. However, by the time this particular vehicle reached RMS it had been re-bodied by Heaver as a 26-seater coach, the body of which would in due course be transferred onto the Gilford chassis of **No.2 (MY 3462**), at which point it also assumed the fleet number 10. This bus was new to W. **King** of Nomansland in 1928 and re-bodied in the mid-1930'ss it was worthwhile.

No.12 (CMO 600). After WW2 began the only single-deck option for new vehicles was the Bedford OWB with its 'utility' style bus body seating 32 on wood-slatted seating, which used the same 28hp petrol engine as the OB-type introduced in 1939. As built they also had quite small headlamps, but most were upgraded and also received coach seating, whilst this one has been rebuilt around the first bay, windscreen and destination indicator, though in the lower view of it, all the original features were still evident, as seen at The Wharf in service. The upper view shows it after sale, when it was a mobile shop for Lawrence Wakerly in Swindon, a fate shared by many other small buses during the mid-1950's, as villages lost their traditional stores. This bus had been new to Reliance in January 1943 and sold in September 1957, note the small headlamps fitted as new.

No.13 (UF 8832) was one of many coaches to be requisitioned for was service, some of which were later released for sale, a useful source of vehicles for rebuilding for further service in the post-war scramble for vehicles. This former *Southdown MS* Leyland 'Tiger' TS4-type of 1932 had a Harrington body when new, but after the chassis was rebuilt by RMS it went to the local Lambourn Coachworks for this new coach body, which saw it survive until 1960, making it a popular sight and engine sound with local enthusiasts!

No.13 (UF 8832) was caught by the camera of Graham Low in 1959, showing the fine order it was kept in, still being used on Private Hire work then, along with the Kennet School contract out of the Brightwalton area. As part of its post-war work on the chassis rebuild it had received this longer 'Cov-Rad' replacement radiator grille to modernise its front end and the mudguards had also been re-modelled, whilst the Lambourn body for 33-seats was built to a traditional look of the time.

Seen again at the end of its active service, the same coach, this photo shows that the body, despite being a one-off, was a good investment. Indeed, that coachbuilder, as with Vincents in Reading, also built very solid horseboxes. To keep this coach going the firm had bought from *Thames Valley* a similar TS3-type to use its engine, the remains being broken up in the orchard for its seats etc.

No.14 (CRX 34) was another Bedford OWB obtained in January 1944, operators having to apply to the Ministry for an allocation, which Reliance was able to get with its public bus routes. It came at a time when the older stock was getting beyond the skills to keep them on the road, with its 32-seater utility body by Duple. Martin Shaw saw it still in original condition, and it was scrapped in November 1952, poor quality timber due to wartime shortages rendering the body past it.

No.15 (CRX 682) was another OWB-type, which arrived in October 1945, when new with a Duple MkII 30-seat bus body, but to extend its life it was sent in 1959 for this Duple 'Vista' 29-seater coach body, caught by local photographer Philip Wallis on an AWRE contract near The Falcon at Tadley. In the second guise as a coach it was based at Newbury and widely used for private hire and contracts, serving the firm through to 1963.

The same vehicle is shown still carrying its original MkII Duple bus body, which was of the relaxed style after the utilities before that, with curved panels and better interior finishes. In that form it was mainly used on the bus services out to Wantage and Cold Ash, through to the decision to send it for re-bodying after its 1958 overhaul. This photo was by Oxford-based R.H.G. Simpson, who operated an approval service by post for many years, with good local coverage of operators.

No.15 (CRX 684) in another view by Ray Simpson is seen with the original body at The Wharf and on the Cold Ash route. Next to it is former *Maidstone & District* AEC 'Regal' No.**45 (DKT 18)**, one of two such buses purchased from that source in order to increase seating capacity on the bus services, well-kept buses which gave many more years of good operation at Reliance, amongst others also on that chassis type for both buses and coaches.

6

No.16 (DJB 406) was the first all-new post-war purchase, being a Bedford OB-type with Duple 'Vista' 29-seater coach body delivered in 1946, the 28hp chassis being found in many coach fleets, large and small, all over the country. One factor was that such a type could cross the old bridge to the ever-popular resort of Hayling Island, to which the Reliance coaches often travelled on the regular excursions from most of the villages around Newbury. However, many early post-war bodies used poor timber, so this coach only lasted until 1959.

No.17 (WN 8978) was another bus obtained to reduce relief workings on the bus services, being a 32-seater by Weymann on a Dennis 'Lancet' MkII chassis, new in 1936 to *South Wales Transport*, coming to Reliance in 1948 and seeing 5 years use. It was seen at The Wharf ready for a journey to Brightwalton, its Dennis petrol engine of 35.7hp being useful when carrying a full load over the Downs, so popular with the drivers!

In another view of **No.17 (WN 8978)** taken By Roy Marshall at The Wharf, we can see the raked steering-wheel column, which on that model protruded through the front dash. The photo also captures a former *Ribble Motor Services* Leyland 'Tiger' with *Newbury & District* and a double-decker of *Venture of Basingstoke*, those two firms then being part of *Red & White*.

7

Another AEC 'Regal' bus was **No.18 (VH 4682)**, a former *Huddersfield CT* example with Northern Counties 32-seater rear-entrance body new in 1932, coming to Reliance in December 195 2and lasting for 5 years before being scrapped, to keep other examples of that chassis type on the road, though this example retained its petrol engine to the end, coming to Brightwalton via the dealer W. North of Leeds. The seating capacity helped reduce the need for reliefs.

No.19 (EBL 430) was very much a repeat order as a Bedford OB with Duple 'Vista' 29-seater coach body new in October 1947. It ran until September 1965, and following the takeover of *John Donovan* of Yattendon it became the regular outstation allocation, which meant being parked at the driver's home for its regular task of the AERE Harwell contract from that location, plus excursions at the weekends, his E&T licenses also adding local passengers.

No.19 (EBL 430) was caught by M. Bateman at The Wharf on 18th July 1962, by which time Reliance had consolidated its range of villages covered by excursions through the acquisition of *Bert Austin* of Cold ash, *Donovan* as noted above and the Newbury-based *Enterprise Coaches*, all including The Wharf as a pick-up. However, on that day it was engaged on covering the bus service up to Wantage.

A number of the 'Regals' in the fleet were coaches with classic styles of bodywork, but a real favourite was the sole example by Vincent of Reading new in 1947 as **No.21 (EJB 584).** It was an 0662-type chassis, whilst the body had a mix of features which harked back to pre-war designs from the coachbuilder better known for its horseboxes. Indeed, it was certainly solidly built, so sometimes a challenge for its 7.7-litre engine. The 'Tiger' **No.13** is seen alongside it here.

Due to the difficulty in obtaining new buses, it had taken *Thames Valley* a few years to finally withdraw many of its pre-war types, so **No.25 (ABL 760)** came to Reliance in 1950, having been rebuilt bodily by *TV* to see 7 years of service. It was a TS7 'Tiger' with 32-seater body by ECW, one of many standard buses purchased in the 1935-8 period to replace various odd types taken over from various independents.

Some smaller chassis makers also tried to fill the shortage of PSV chassis in the early post-war period, Commer offering this 23A-type, which Reliance took in 1950 as **No.24 (FMO 145)**, fitted with a 33-seater body by Strachans, part of the range of 'Avenger'-type chassis which enjoyed a brief following. It was photographed by Reliance for use in publicity of the time, being a prime private hire coach until ousted by the Burlingham 'Seagulls' on AEC 'Reliance chassis.

No.26 (GJB 491) was on the post-war SB-type design, which replaced the OB, fitted with a Duple 'Vega' body seating 33 and delivered in 1951. It duly developed some structural problems and was thoroughly rebuilt by Reliance, something it was well capable of undertaking. At the time of this Philip Wallis photo it was allocated to Yattendon outstation, the hose-pipe in the foreground being part of the 'facilities' there.

The coach spent much of its time prior to the rebuild of 1956 on private hire and day excursions, shown here in a typical coach park at an unknown destination. The rebuild extended its working life, so it was not withdrawn until November 1963, when it took the short journey up to Mary Hare School for the Deaf over at Snelsmore Common, though it continued to be maintained by Reliance, the first of several coaches sold to that location in fact over the years.

In addition to the previous comments on this coach, one of the very popular aspects of Reliance was the seasonal express service to Southsea, which took its passengers from various villages and then called at The Wharf and Winchester. Roy Marshall saw it in this view after it had replaced No.19 (EBL 430) as the Yattendon allocation on that express service. Most Reliance excursions also left from that area, so the scene could be a busy one, what with the service buses all in brown and cream!

No.23 (ERX 284) was mostly another repeat order for an OB with 'Vista' 29-seater body by Duple, but it was fitted with a 4-cylinder Perkins diesel engine, as signified by the badge on the radiator grille. That type was found to be economic and easy to maintain, so this coach was extensively used, even being sent to the Blackpool Illuminations, and was also a regular choice for the Sunday operations to Brightwalton and Wantage, or when there was snow on The Downs!

The same coach is seen on a Wantage journey, and after the full fleetname had been replaced by an 'R' set in a circle on the body side. It put in a full 20 years with the firm before being sold onto *Kingdom* of Tiverton, shown here with Duple (Midland)-bodied **No.73 (NTH 690)** in the background headed for Brightwalton so the photo was taken sometime between 1961 and 1966.

No.27 (JB 7499) was another former *Thames Valley* Leyland 'Tiger' TS7-type, but with a Brush body seating 35. In this view it had been hired to taake a party of Boy Scouts for their Annual Camp, being well loaded with all their equipment, whilst they all seemed to be keen to appear in the photo! Over the years, the firm must have carried virtually everyone in the area to some event or another, as in the days before widespread private car ownership all public events attracted big crowds.

No.28 (HON 623) was one of a succession of secondhand coaches based on the AEC 'Regal' chassis series, whilst next to it is the equivelant double-decker on a 'Regent' type. The coach had a 9621A-type chassis with powerful 9.6-litre engine, and the location is the Mill Lane yard taken over with the business of *Enterprise Coaches* of Newbury, which formed the allocation in that town before the new garage in Boundary Road was built.

Another view of that same coach shows off the lines of the Burlingham bodywork of this 33-seater, mostly used for contract duties and driven by a Chargehand Fitter, so it also went up to Brightwalton at times. It came to Reliance in 1952 and was sold again in 1964, being used for sometime on the run to the Royal Ordnance Stores at Didcot. The top photo was by Ray Simpson and the lower one by Bob Mack of Leeds who often visited the area.

No.29 (NRE 234) was a used example of the OB with Duple 'Vista' body acquired when 5 years old in 1952, having been new to *Greatrex* of Stafford. It is recalled by Dave Wilder as the least reliable of its type, though for some time it covered the RAF Welford run and some coastal excursions. This photo taken 12th July 1959 by an un-named person was likely done whilst he was on a lay-over on an express service through The Wharf that day?

No.29 (NRE 234) is seen again at The Wharf, but on a Brightwalton service trip, with the Vincent-bodied AEC 'Regal' coach **No.21 (EJB 584)** parked next to it.

After the Bedford OB was withdrawn in December 1959 is was officially scrapped, though the process could be a lengthy one starting with being parked in the orchard. Several photos showing the process appear on page 92, such vehicles keeping others of their type on the road for longer.

No.30 (HRX 10) was a significant addition to the fleet, bringing with it the 'Seagull' body design by the Blackpool coachbuilder Burlingham, though in its case the 'Baby' version for use on front-engine chassis. It is seen in a 1964 Philip Wallis photo at Winchester Coach Station, out on the By-pass in order to reduce through traffic, complete with cafeteria and bar. As new it was registered JRX 10 in error, but never ran in that form, the livery by then having change to this style, though the paint colours remained the same.

This offside view of **No.30 (HRX 10)** by Thomas W.W. Knowles shows off the neat lines of the Burlingham coachwork. However, in its original form as a petrol-engined SB-type, it was found to be heavy on fuel, so was used on a Harwell run and left there all day, but in 1963 it was changed to a diesel SB1 with the Bedford diesel engine, after which it was more widely used.

No.32 (EFC 286) was one of a number AEC 'Regal' saloons purchased to increase capacity on the bus services, seen alongside a former *Thames Valley* 'Tiger' It had been new to *City of Oxford MS* in April 1937, that firm having a good reputation for high maintenance. With a 34-seater body by Weymann it came to Reliance in April 1959. It was usually found on the Brightwalton route, but shown on a snowy day bound for Cold Ash.

No.32 (EFC 286) is seen again on the stands for the service routes at The Wharf in a photo by R. Gingell. The 'camel-back body style was typical of those built for BET Federation operators in the 1930's, and it is seen in company with other 'Regal' saloons **No.50 (CVT 684)** and **No.44 (DKT 25)**, which came from *Potteries MT* and *Maidstone & District,* the latter still wearing the liveries they had been acquired in, though repainted in due course into the brown and cream livery.

No.23 (EFC 285) was the other of the pair emanating from Oxford, shown in this Roy Marshall photo on the Cold Ash stand. After withdrawal in 1955 it was scrapped for spares, though over at *Smith's of Reading* their former *COMS* 'Regals' were re-bodied for longer working lives, some with bodies actually older than the chassis, albeit fully refurbished. Neither of the pair bought by Reliance saw any subsequent owners, but their parts lived on in keeping others going.

Alan Cross saw **No.32 (EFC 286)** at Ascot Races in June when on hire to *Thames Valley* to cover for delayed delivery of new double-deckers that year. The *City of Oxford* livery was a nice but complex one, harking back to tramway days with maroon, red and duck egg blue! The AEC 7.7 diesel engine of these buses was a most notably reliable unit, and of course COMS was a neighbour of Reliance, also with its own contracts to the Harwell and Didcot areas, some double-deckers from that fleet following in due course, as we shall see.

However, the next generation of AECs was quite different, with the move to underfloor-engined designs, along with a new standard of coachwork soon to be seen on top duties with Reliance. **No.34 (JRX 867**) was on the aptly-names 'Reliance' chassis, and fitted with a 41-seater 'Seagull' design body by Burlingham, given the registration HRX 867 in error when new in May 1954. It gave 18 years of excellent service on private hires and excursions, used from Brightwalton until 1962, when transferred to the Newbury allocation for a couple more years on the contracts. The centre-doorway layout was quite common on this style of body, making the front nearside pair of seats a popular vantage point for passengers. Both these views are by Ray Simpson of Oxford, and the coach was very much liked by drivers with its 7.685-litre engine and vacuum brakes.

No.35 (ABL 757) was also a former *Thames Valley* TS7-type 'Tiger' 35-seater with ECW body new in 1937, coming to Reliance in 1955, but only retained for a couple of years. It is seen at The Wharf working the bus service to Wantage, a point reached by TV from Reading for many years on its Route 5A, a bus having been outstationed there ever since the 1920's in various locations. It had a thorough body rebuild around 1950.

The success of the initial 'Reliance' led to an order for **No.36 (LBL 197)** in May 1955, though as built it had a front-entrance, which had been altered during repairs following a bad smash with an Army lorry near Weymouth, so became centre-door as shown here. Its driver Tony Smith had the presence of mind to shout a warning to those on board that day, which kept to a minimum any injuries in that accident, and it was rebuilt back at Blackpool by Burlingham. The scene is Hastings Coach Park, with the east Cliff Lift as the backdrop, a point still used by coaches to this day.

In the lower view we see it again at The Wharf, next to a Guy underfloor-engine coach on an express service, and indeed the coach was often to be found on the Reliance express to the ever-popular South Coast resort Southsea taking many 1000's on day trips or for longer breaks on the nearby Isle of Wight. Newbury was a stop-over point on many express services east-to-west and north-to-south for decades.

No.36 (LBL 197) was one of a trio of native AEC 'Reliances', all of which had long working lives. Martin Shaw took this photo on 4th June 1963 at Oxford's Gloucester Green Bus Station, where the bus and express coach services into the city had been based from the 1930's. Although the author never rode on the Reliance examples, he does recall the splendid rides on *Brimblecombe Bros.* KMO 939 with 'Seagull' body, as well as the Duple-bodied examples at *Smith's Coaches of Reading,* all of which lasted many years.

Another type familiar to the author through the fleets of *Brimblecombes, Smith's* and *Gough's Garage* in his Bracknell base was the Duple 'Vista-bodied Bedford OB, on many an outing or seaside expresses.

Reliance **No.38 (HOB 941)** had come into the fleet through the acquisition of *Donovan* of Yattendon in May 1955, but had been new to Birmingham-based operator *Burleys* in July 1947. Standing next to it is a similar coach (CWV 999) of *Rimes* of Swindon, a firm from which Reliance would duly buy a couple of coaches. The Yattendon take-over had provided a number of useful licenses to add to the excursions pick-ups, that business earlier having been the *Donovan & Crane* partnership, with its origins in a Country Carrier service, as indeed were a number of local concerns. This coach was kept until November 1962, when it was scrapped for spares to live on in other OB-types.

No.41 (DDL 924) had been new to *Weavell* of Newport on the Isle of Wight in January 1946, but reached the Reliance fleet via *Perdue* of Hungerford in 1955. The Duple MkII body had been re-seated to 29 using former *LTE* seats, and was notable for its in-built luggage racks from its Island days catering for the holidaymakers. It is seen at The Wharf in 1958 on one of the service routes, being sold in 1959 to become a mobile shop in Surrey.

No.42 (ETM 649) was one of a pair of Guy 'Arab' MkIII's with Gardner 5LW engines acquired in late 1955. Whilst something of a departure for Reliance, it joined many others of that type in Newbury working for *N&D,* including those drafted there from the *Thames Valley* fleet for the ease of maintenance under the care of Garage Foreman Reg Hibbert, who could always be relied on if Reliance ever needed help with its examples, both of which originated with Bartle of *Potton* in 1946, passing to *United Counties* through takeover. These were mainly used on contracts, but did sometimes appear on the services, as here with **No.43 (ETM 650)** on the route to Brightwalton. It was sold in September 1960 to Frank Pelham, showman of Hurst, near Wokingham, the show people much liking the 5LW engine, which was a very reliable unit from that Manchester-based engine-builder. Note the *Wilts & Dorset* Bristol KSW-type next to it in on the Salisbury service.

No.44 (DKT 25) was one of a pair of Harrington-bodied AEC 'Regal' 0662-types of 1937 new to *Maidstone & District,* coming to Reliance in June 1956, and it stayed until November 1959, used as a general workhorse on contracts, and occasionally on the service routes, where the 34-seater capacity was useful. In this photo taken by Ray Simpson it was caught on the Wantage route with a good load, so quite likely on a market day. The service to that old Berkshire town was reduced over the years, so at the time of the sale of the routes it was discontinued, with another old link lost.

No.46 (MJB 820) was the third of the 'Seagull'-bodied 'Reliance coaches, arriving in May 1956 with a centre-entrance layout and seating 41, its lines suiting the application of the livery, indeed a classic design of its era. It was found at the popular Kent Coast resort of Margate, though as with the others of its type, most often was on the busy Southsea express service, as in the lower offside view at the large Coach Park provided since the 1920's by the City of Portsmouth, which greatly assisted in attracting coach traffic to the growing resort, along with its pier, fun-fair and of course the ferry connections to the Isle of Wight, all of which along with the Naval Dockyards and its historic ships kept that destination one of the most popular through to the present day. It was where *Charlie Durnford* ran his pioneering 'chara' outing!

No.47 (ABE 957) was another 'Regal' 0662-type, but with a rare body built by Barnaby of Hull, new in June 1938 to the legendry Scunthorpe-based operator *Enterprise & Silver Dawn,* passing with them to the *Lincolnshire Road Car Co.*, then via others to reach Reliance in 1956, where it stayed for 6 years, having had an extensive body over haul on arrival, which saw the seating increased from 32 to 37, making it a useful bus on busy service routes. In the top photo Graham Low saw it at The Wharf on a run to Brightwalton and Chaddleworth, but next we see it at Brightwalton depot in a photo by Paul White, who visited relatives in the area regularly. The rebuild left it looking like a Plaxton production, and it replaced Thurgood-bodied Guy 'Arab' No.43 (ETM 650) as the regular Brightwalton route bus. It was only taken out of service due to being unsuitable for adaption for one-man-operation, so it was reluctantly withdrawn.

No. 49 (HYF 971) was one of a number of secondhand Bedford OBs with Duple 'Vista' 29-seater coach bodies acquired during the 1950's. It had started out with *British South American Airways* in April 1947, based in London W1, but actually came to the firm when it acquired the *Whutchurch Motor Company,* who contributed similar coach No.48 (TMY 941), new to the *Middlesex Hospital.* It was used generally on private hires and contracts, being withdrawn in late 1963.

No.50 (CVT 684) was yet another 'Regal' variant, a scarce MkII which had the the 6.6-litre engine as new, but subsequent replacement by the standard 7.7-litre unit resulted in the slightly protruding radiator, which can be discerned in the offside view. It had been new to *Brown* of Tunstall, who had sold out to *Potteries Motor Traction* un due course, and was new in March 1936 with a Duple body seating 39, though reduced to 35 with *PMT*. It was regarded by Reliance as under-powered, certainly not up to the Wantage route, so left after a relatively short time in December 1959, after just short of 3 years of use. Who took the top photo is unrecorded, but Graham Low found it at The Wharf on one of his regular visits there, both views confirming it was a permanent fixture on the Cold Ash route, but stylish enough in its general look.

No.51 (CN 9547) was in order to meet the requirement for double-deckers on the Harwell and Aldermaston contracts. As with *Smiths of Reading*, the initial purchases were former *London Transport* types, but then the net was spread wider to find further AEC 'Regents', standard of course with the number of 'Regals' already in the fleet. This example started life in May 1940 with the *Northern General* fleet, n 0661-type with 56-seater highbridge Weymann body, coming to Reliance in March 1957, based at the Newbury outstation for contracts, but sometimes also on service reliefs.

21

No. 53 (CWV 430) was an interesting purchase from a nearby operator, being new to *Rimes* of Swindon in July 1942 as a utility-bodied Bedford OWB-type. However, it had been re-bodied by Lee Coachworks of Bournemouth in 1948 with this vaguely lookalike of the Duple 'Vista' coach body, but with a deeper roof-line and rather upright side profile. Indeed, all 4 coaches acquired from Rimes had a specific story, many operators resorting to re-bodying when wartime bodies started to deteriorate due to the poor quality of timber used and shortages of skilled craftsmen when then they were constructed.

This coach came to Reliance in December 1957 and stayed until May 1964, generally used on Newbury-based contracts, later becoming a worker's bus for a construction firm, a common for many old coaches in that era. The style of the windows was odd around the first bay, but otherwise passed for an OB.

No.54 (HYP 722) was indeed a standard Bedford OB with Duple 'Vista' 29-seater coach body, acquired by the firm in December 1957 and retained until May 1965. It had started out with North London operator *Birch Bros.,* a well-known source of good used coaches, and it was sent to the Yattendon outstation as replacement for No.38 (HOB 941) in November 1962, and was generally used on private hires due to its superior interior finish as specified.

No.54 (HYP 722) is seen again in a photo by David Gillard at Southsea Coach Park. Apart from the main attractions of that resort and the neighbouring Dockyard, it also generated many passengers travelling on to the Isle of Wight for a long holiday, a side variety of accommodation available on the Island. Indeed, Smiths of Reading found that was so much the case that it introduced a second journey back from Southsea to cater better for those coming off the ferries apart from the day-trippers returning home – clever use of the same coach, but a very busy day for its driver!

No.55 (EGB 184) was an AEC 'Regal' MkIII 0962-type chassis with a Duple A-type body new in July 1947 to *Northern Roadways* of Glasgow. It passed to *Rimes* of Swindon, then to reliance in December 1957. Having the more powerful 9.6-litre engine it operated on everything out of Newbury outstation until withdrawn and scrapped in early 1963, its body and mechanical parts keeping other similar coaches on the road, and in particular such items as body mouldings and glazing to be used for repair of accidental damage.

No.56 (EWV 396) was also the same specification, but had been supplied new to *Rimes* in November 1947, arriving with the coach above in December 1957. It had a 33-seater body which duly developed bulkhead weakness due to the use of poor timber when built, that year not being a good one!

No.57 (BUS 168) was one of a number of former *Glasgow Corporation* buses to add to the double-deck fleet for contract operations. It was an AEC 'Regent' 0661-type with 7.7-litre oil engine new in Jne 1938. When built it had a Cowieson body, but many buses of that period for that operator went through a re0bodying programme, so in 1950 it received this 56-seater body by Scottish Aviation, a WW2 plane-maker going over to PSVs.

No.58 (HWJ 991) had been new to the *Sheffield United Tours* fleet, an AEC 'Regal' 0662-type with 7.7-litre engine and Duple A-type body with superior interior finish delivered in September 1949. Despite that, it is recalled as the least reliable of the type with the firm, coming to them in January 1959. It was used mainly on contracts and private hire out of Brightwalton garage, but after withdrawal in November 1962 its better seats went into similar coach No.81 (HXB 457), which arrived soon after that and was subject to a lot of work prior to entering active service. The top view of it is by Roy Marshall, whose photos now form part of The Bus Archive, he always had a soft spot for the Reliance fleet and indeed the Independents in general. The lower view is by locally-based (at that time) Peter Wilks, who worked for *Thames Valley*, but was a frequent visitor to Newbury. *Sheffield United Tours* were pioneers of extended tours to Continental Europe.

No.58 (HWJ 991) is seen in another Roy Marshall view as it swings out of Newbury Wharf, the Bus Station having been laid out on the old filled-in basin of the Kennet & Avon Canal in the 1920s as part of moves to reduce congestion in the Market Place, initially for the use of the Carrier's vans. The Old Granary on the left was even older and by then housed the Enquiry Office for *Thames Valley* (ex-*Newbury & District*) to the left of the coach, other shops and cafes, with the office for Reliance at the far end. In the background is the tower of the Victorian Town Hall over the Market Place area.

No.59 (CRP 300) was also a Duple-bodied AEC 'Regal' 0662-type new in June 1946 to Northampton-based *York Bros.*, coming to Reliance in March 1959, but only staying until October 1961. It duly replaced No.50 (CVT 684) as the regular Cold Ash bus, but although mechanically it was very sound, the body did suffer from soft timber issues, which shortened its stay. After that it remained in the scrapyard of Rush Green Motors, where it slowly rotted away. Also, of course, once the newer types of coaches came around, the half-cab models became rather dated in looks and were not suited to one-man-operation for use on the bus services, so were to be found mainly on the contracts and lesser hires such as school outings. The upper photo was by Graham Low and the lower one by Ray Simpson at The Wharf.

Believe it or not, **No.60 (SME 84)** was another 0662-type 'Regal', though only the AEC roundel set in the 'wings' on the front end even hints at that! It had been a Brush 32-seater when new, but in 1954 was re-bodied by original owners *Venture Transport* of London NW2 with this Duple 'Vega'-style 35-seat body of a type developed for use on such models as the Commer 'Avenger' range, After coming to the firm in 1959 it ran in the former owner's yellow and black scheme for a time, not being particularly widely used, mostly on contracts based on Brightwalton. The upper view by Philip Wallis from November 1962 is a rare one to include the *RMS* garage at Brightwalton, with its stepped-gable front elevation. It rarely strayed much away from that area, but conversely the lower photo by Thomas W.W. Knowles taken in 1960 does sat least prove it went to Portsmouth on that day, perhaps a dedicated 'relief' coach from its usual base?

Thomas also found the more conventional example of Duple A-type-bodied **No.61 (OMX 325)** parked in the centre of the wide road notably in the centre of Marlborough, one of a number of photos he took when based in that area. It had also started out with *Venture Transport* in 1950, but by then supplies of sound timber had improved. It was the 09621A-type, so with its larger engine, it was widely used on excursions, private hires and longer contracts.

Although not a colour photo as such, there is good reason to think when Martin Shaw saw **No.61 (OMX 325)** it still wore the black and yellow livery of former owner *Venture Transport*. It was seen on 30th April 1960 at Oxford's Bus station at Gloucester Green. It had a good reputation for being a reliable coach, dealing with all tasks assigned to it until withdrawn in May 1964, after which it had several further PSV operators.

No.63 (LPA 952) came from another well-known Independent of many years standing, *Surrey Motors* of Sutton, which had a livery of yellow and brown, a nice scheme for a well-kept fleet. New in June 1947, it was an 0662-type 'Regal' with Harrington 33-seater body. It arrived at reliance in October 1959, but David Wilder recalled that it was not in great condition compared with its twin, but it was re-engined with the 7.7-litre unit from No.21 (EJB 584). David Gillard saw it outside the mill Lane shed, assigned to contracts through to withdrawal in November 1963.

On the other hand, **No.64 (LPA 951)** was in much neater shape, shown here in a Roy Marshall shot of it at The Wharf covering the bus service to Wantage. It was more generally found on private hire, but as fate would have it, a bad smash with an American car whilst working a relief at Chapel Arch on the Wantage route led to a twisted chassis and it was withdrawn after that accident in May 1961.

No.65 (JTX 667) was a MkIII 9621E-type 'Regal', but this time with a typical Burlingham 33-seater body of its new date of 1950, to *Edwards* of Beddell, coming to Reliance in early 1960 for a stay of little over 4 years, Having been fully refurbished before purchase, it was put to work on coaching duties at weekends, but covered the Royal Ordnance Depot run to Didcot, combined with the Compton School contract throughout the week. The plain front dash of the Burlingham body is more apparent in this nearside view. It is shown in a Ray Simpson photo by the mill Lane shed, that area having many years of local operator connections, and came into the reliance fold with the *Enterprise Coaches* purchase. Further back was the original *Thames Valley* Dormy Shed from the 1920's, whilst *Red & White* had re-equipped *Newbury & District* with a new garage postwar, making that area full of local history relevant to transport, the *Enterprise* shed once being the base for the *Durnford & Sons* haulage and removals vehicles. In the lowest photo we see the same coach as it emerges into Cheap Street from Kings Road, which had been the original base for *Denham Bros.,* pioneering bus operators in Newbury and one of the original partners in *Newbury & District Motor Services* when formed in 1932. George Hedges joined with that firm that year, but left after a disagreement in 1934!

No.66 (BGA 19) was another former *Glasgow CT* AEC 'Regent' 0661-type new in October 1937, when it had a Cowieson 56-seater body, receiving this body by Alexanders in 1950 with the same capacity. It came south in November 1959 and had a platform door added around 1962 due to windy conditions on the Berkshire Downs. It was given the engine from No.64 (LPA 951) following its premature withdrawal, and was noted as a reliable vehicle, staying until early 1965 on contract duties.

This second view of the same bus by Ray Simpson sees it on a rarer outing on a private hire job, which at times might warrant a double-decker, particularly for football supporters, but otherwise its mainstay was the Aldermaston contract to AWRE from Newbury, and when in the Bus Park could be seen alongside double-deckers from the Reading-based Smith's Coaches also on contracts to that site, the workforce being drawn from a very wide area from Wokingham in the east out as far as Hungerford and Aldbourne to the west.

No.67 (VMO 440) contrasts with the types used mainly on the contracts, as it was new in July 1960 as a 'Reliance' chassis carrying a 41-seater Duple 'Britannia'-style body. Indeed, the blind set to 'Reliance' no doubt caused Phil Moth to smile when he found it parked by the seaside. The popular South Coast resorts were often served, along with the Kent and Essex Coasts.

No.67 (VMO 440) ran in this plainer livery until a full re-paint was due. It was the flagship coach of the Newbury allocation and used on all top-notch work until cascading to contracts in the mid-60's. Alf Smith over at Reading noted his Duple-bodied 'Reliances' were the best coaches he ever had, and this example served Reliance through to July 1975, then moving on to *Reed* of Maidenhead for further service. This photo was by Thomas W.W. Knowles, a regular visitor.

The opportunity arose in September 1960 to acquire this just over 5 year-old 41-seater 'Reliance' with Duple 'Elizabethan'-style body. **No.68 (PAD 587)** had been new to *Miller* based at Cirencester, continuing to run in their green livery for some time, known locally as 'the green coach', its specification and centre-entrance body fitting in nicely with the native examples. It was based at Brightwalton for all front-line duties, until later cascaded onto contracts.

It was duly given full livery, but the 'M' monogram on the body sides was changed to an 'R' as was then appearing on other vehicles in the fleet. Some of the excursions ran to Southend-on-Sea, quite a run from the west of the area served by Reliance, and the coach was caught there on 8th June 1968, in company with No.104 (DRX 748C). It was duly withdrawn in June 1971 and went on to have 4 further owners in Wales!

No.69 (LUY 750) was yet another old 'Regal' 0662-type, though not looking like this when new in March 1938 as EHW 532 to *Bristol Tramways* with a Duple half-cab coach body. It passed to dealer and coachbuilders Yeates based at Loughborough, who extended the chassis and built this dual-purpose 39-seater body before re-registering it in 1953. After several owners it came to Reliance in 1960, and in the course of a body rebuild it was fitted with the radiator grille from an AEC 'Mercury' lorry. It was also unusual inside for having a large glass panel as the front bulkhead and a blue finish. However, the body was rather heavy for the 7.7-litre engine, so it was sold in October 1965, caught here by the camera of Philip Wallis, a regular visitor to Newbury, as it was readied for a trip to Swanage. Paul White was another regular visitor to the area as he had relatives there, and fortunately took a number of views of Reliance stock, including this one of the rebuilt and re-bodied AEC 'Regal' as outlined above, on that occasion going to Wantage.

No.70 (208 BRE) carries one stage of the Duple 'Vega' body referred to as the 'oval grille', new in 1954 and reaching Reliance in 1960, it seated 36 due to the maximum length of coaches increasing to 30ft. It later received a double rear window After No.65 (JTX 667) ran into the back of it near The Downs School in 1963.

No.71 (219 BRE) despite being a 'twin' to No.70, had a much nicer interior, so it duly transferred to Boundary Road Garage when that opened. Both of those coaches started with Corvedale of Ludlow and stayed at Reliance until 1965, seeing general use on all coaching activities. Note the different tone on the area around the 'R' monogram circle, caused by the reflection of a short-lived body variant using a polished area to the 'Vega'.

Left to right No.100 (939 ARP), No.101 (775 CD) No.102 (796 BOR) and No.72 (329 ABJ) comprised all of the quartet of minibuses owned when Ray Simpson visited the depot. 72 was based at the Brightwalton Garage and kept very busy, ehereas the other trio were for the specific use on the contract to the School of Military Survey at Hermitage, where incidently the author completed his City & Guilds Advanced Litho Printing Practical Test on a 1930's Crabtree press!

No.73 (NTH 690) would be the first of a number of similar service saloons using the Duple (Midland) 40-seater body on Bedford SBO chassis, being new to *Davis* of Pentcader in 1956. It was decided to convert the Brightwalton and Wantage routes to o-m-o working prior to its arrival in September 1961, though the Cold Ash route was considered too busy for such operation. It was often on Brightwalton services, and also trips to Wantage.

The author visited Newbury regularly during the 1960's, one of the main attractions being the former *Newbury & District* Guy 'Arab' MkIII double-deckers. Visits usually started at The Wharf, then round to Mill Lane Garage to see Reg Hibbert, followed by going around the corner into the Reliance Garage, and on some days the afternoon would see him jump on the 112 up to Oxford to check on South Midland at Botley Road, then Route 5 back to Reading and the 2 home to Bracknell! Guy H10 (FMO 517) is seen here along with **No.73 (NTH 690)**, one of the Duple (Midland)-bodied Bedford SB's that served Reliance on the bus routes for many years. The top photo is by Philip Wallis, but it was Peter Trevaskis who caught the same bus in the Market Place at Wantage in late 1961 awaiting the return to Newbury. When the author rode to that town on TV's Route 5A from Reading he had no idea of his family connections there going back to the early 1800's, an Eaton forebear working as an ostler in the hotel behind the bus.

No.74 (YMO 324) represented the state of affairs of the Duple 'Super Vega' body, when it was new on a Bedford SB1 chassis in August 1961. It also included some blue beading in addition to the red inserts, and it was sent to Yattendon for its first 5 years, used on excursions and private hire at the weekends.

No.75 (NUY 331) came to Reliance in August 1961 to assist in the conversion of some of the bus services to one-man-operation, though initially it was used with a crew on the Cold Ash route, before going onto Wantage and Brightwalton runs. It was new in October 1954 to *Yarrenton* of Tetbury Wells and was the only one of the quartet of similar buses to have moquette-covered bus seats. The is photo by another Newbury visitor Ray Simpson, whilst the lower shot is by locally-based Philip Wallis, whose job took him all over West Berkshire and North Hampshire, fortunately he carried his camera with him and recorded much of the transport scene of that era. He also caught the buses and coaches at AWRE and Harwell, as well as those visiting through the protest marches organised by CND. The *Thames Valley* Enquiry Office was the first door on the left of The Wharf, whilst the Reliance office was at the far end.

No.76 (OLD 142) was a 36-seater added to the fleet to fulfil the role for smaller hires and contracts in early 1962. It had been new in 1954 to *Grey-Green* up in North London and carried a body by Harrington on a Bedford SBO chassis. It was seen in George Street in Oxford by Ray Simpson as it passed the Oxford Theatre, a regular excursion venue for Reliance all year round, but especially during the pantomime season, when numerous parties of youngsters and their parents booked many seats.

No.76 (OLD 142) evidently did get to stretch its legs at times, being seen here at the Winchester Coach Station by Philip Wallis, probably bound for the South Coast, though Reliance coaches rarely displayed their intended destination, even though this coach had a full roll fitted, as the author found on a similar example with *Smith's of Reading*! Then again it could be a private job, as the firm had a very wide patronage throughout West Berkshire though the years of serving all the local groups, churches and schools.

Another Philip Wallis photo gives us two Duple-bodied SB's at The Wharf, with **No.75 (NUY 331)** and **No.80 (SX 8901)** working the Cold Ash and Wantage services in 1962. It was this pair used on the final day, and a view taken on that occasion appears on page 96, as a tribute to over 4 decades of service to the local population.

No.64 LPA 951) takes us back a little, with one of a pair of Harrington-bodied AEC 'Regal' 0662-types acquired in 1959 from *Surrey Motors* of Sutton, new to them in 1947 and finished in their yellow and brown livery. However, this coach had its career ended early due to a collision with a large American car in August 1961, which although did not damage the body much, fatally bent the chassis frame, so it was duly scrapped, with the engine going into former *Glasgow CT* AEC 'Regent' No.66 (BGA 19)

No.72 (329 ABJ) filled the role of a minibus, at a time when coaches were getting even larger, and it was kept very busy out of its base at Brightwalton all week on contracts and private hires, being new in 1958 to *Sharman* of Oxford and acquired in 1961. On arrival it had a green and cream livery which it retained for some time, later moving to Newbury until sold in June 1969. It is parked outside the Reliance office at No.1 The Wharf, with displays for excursions shown in the windows, other buildings being cafes, shops etc.

No. 77 (AEY 175) was a 36-seater on a Bedford SB chassis, but this time by Plaxton, new in 1954 to *Jones* of Llanfet Hill, coming to Reliance in October 1961, and sold again in 1965. Plaxton was then a very minor outfit in the British market for coachbuilding, but its introduction of the 'Panorama' series would alter its fortunes greatly, and we shall see many more later examples of its work over the progress of this review of the Reliance fleet.

The same coach is seen from the nearside in a view by Oxford-based enthusiast Martin Shaw in November 1962 in a Coach Park. Note the Burlingham 'Seagull'-bodied coach behind, and similar examples would in due course grace the fleet. Its body largely resembles the Duple 'Bella Vega', but with hints of Harrington as applied to front-engined chassis types. It led a fairly uneventful life with Reliance on general duties.

No.78 (DCK 219) was an exception to the general progress of coach body designs of the period, and the more usual types being acquired by Reliance! One of a fleet of special double-deck coaches built for the express services of *Ribble Motor Services*, it was a 1951 Leyland 'Titan' PD2/3 carrying an East Lancs 49-seater body as their 'White Lady' coaches. It was new with a rear platform door and came in October 1962, but when sold in 1966 it became re-united with old batchmates at *Premier Travel* over at Cambridge.

In the second view also taken by Graham Low, we can clearly see the platform door and body embellishments, plus the typical *Ribble*-style front destination aperture, which the new owner fitted with a single-line blind. Despite its glorious origins, it was used daily on the contract from Newbury to AWRE Aldermaston, though it did at times go out on private hires or even a service relief! A colour view of this interesting vehicle can be found on page 60.

No.79 (453 BMO) was a far more conventional affair as a 'twin' for No.74 (YMO 324), new in July 1962 with Duple 'Super Vega 41-seat body on Bedford SB5 chassis. It even followed a similar pattern as that coach, with initial allocation to Yattendon to replace a vehicle taken over from *John Donovan*, staying there for about 2 years for contracts to Harwell, seen there in 1964.

No.79 (453 BM0) was also to be seen at Oxford, shown here in this view outside the *South Midland* café at the Gloucester Green Bus Station, maybe laid over during an excursion to the adjacent theatre, Oxford FC or even between contracts. Other coaches ran to the area for Blenheim Palace tours or in the evenings for the Speedway at Cowley. In this shot it has a coach from *Smith's of Reading* next door, the drivers no doubt catching up over a fry-up!

No.80 (SX 8901) as already noted, was a Bedford SBO with Duple (Midland) body, found ideal for the service routes, so Reliance was lucky to buy a pair which had previously been staff buses for Scottish Oils at Uphall, which seated 40. This example ran almost exclusively on the Cold Ash route, which remained as crew-operated after the other 2 had gone over to one-man, due to higher loadings. It had a high-ratio rear axle and was a very fast machine!

It is seen again on the usual duty, awaiting departure from The Wharf, a far cry from the West Lothian area where it had previously operated, though some work needed to be done to meet full PSV standards due to their use for staff. The Midland coach factory of Duple was in Kegworth as successor to Nudd & Lockyer and its bus body was a popular choice with many independents, being simple to maintain and other examples in Berkshire ran for *Blue Bus* of Slough and *Imperial* of Windsor.

No.81 (HXB 457) was another AEC 'Regal' 0662-type with the Duple A-type 35-seater body, new in 1946 to London SE18-based operator *Bradshaw,* coming to Reliance in 1961, but stored at Brightwalton for several years, allowing a thorough body overhaul as it had poor timber, then a re-paint, during which time parts from withdrawn Nos. 58 (HWJ 991) and 59 (CRP 300) were used to complete its entry into service. As the half-cab layout was by then becoming rather dated, it only ran for about 5 years.

No.82 (SX 8902) is shown out on service making its way through the lanes up to Cold Ash, the timetable being used by Philip Wallis to create this sylvan scene. Much of the area was made up of large parkland estates hence the impressive trees lining the road, whilst the fathers of both George Hedges and Albert Austin had made their livings as local workers in the woods, many bowl-turners and hurdle-makers also being listed on the census pages.

No.83 (TEL 700) reminds us that mention was made earlier of Continental style influences on British coach design, and this 1956 AEC 'Reliance' with Plaxton 'Consort' body had sought to present such a difference when ordered by Excelsior of Bournemouth, which had many tours travelling to Europe. The windows and glazed roof lights were to give good landscape views in mountainous regions. To Reliance in 1963, for several years it was used for the Reading FC Supporters.

No.83 (TEL 700) arrived in the plain cream livery of its former owner, and although their holidays were popular they were not cheap when compared with the package tours by air then becoming available. It was in fact not uncommon to see coaches on lay-over sat The Wharf for extended tours, some even headed for Europe via the improved ferry facilities then being introduced on some cross-Channel routes. However, the era of such ventures by Reliance was still some time away.

Another coach displaying similar influences was another AEC 'Reliance' as **No.84 (LVA 271)**, which had been new in 1955 to *Park's* of Strathevan, carrying a 'Venturer MkIII'-style 41-seater body by Plaxton, though it came from another *Reliance* based at Meppershall in a two-tone pink livery, applied to appeal to the ladies it would seem. It had vacuum braking and arrived in 1963 for a 5-year stay.

The above photo was taken by Martin Shaw in 1964, but the lower view was by Ray Simpson at an unknown date. The centre-entrance layout was popular for touring, giving a clearer view from the forward seats, but with Reliance this coach was mostly used on lesser private hires and contracts. It remained in the fleet until 1968, when sold to *Thomas* of Clydebach Vale, quiet a number of coaches from the fleet ending up with operators in Wales. Body styles such as these were duly developed into the early 'Panorama'.

No.86 (MWL 978) was one of a pair of former *City of Oxford* AEC 'Regent' 0661-types purchased in May/June 1963 to replace similar ex-*Glasgow* double-deckers No.62 (BGA 9) and 66 (BGA 19), taking over their duties on contract runs from Newbury to AWRE, along with some occasional relief runs on the services. They had Weymann 56-seater bodies, both of which duly received platform doors, though No.85 (MWL 977) got its when at *Smith's of Reading* prior to coming to Newbury. This photo is from April 1967 taken by the author, the bus leaving the fleet in 1968.

No.87 (504 EBL) is one of the few former Reliance vehicles to survive, in the collection of the Science Museum after donation by the family on withdrawal after 21 years of service. It was their only Bedford VAL, that chassis developed with twin-steer to accommodate this 53-seater body by Duple. As new it was usually driven by a family member such was its novelty locally, but maybe one day this scene at The Wharf can be re-created?!

Martin Shaw caught the 1963 coach in the October of that year as it arrived at Oxford. The 17-inch wheels of the design led to braking deficiencies, which required very frequent adjustment, but the other aim of creating a level floor-line was achieved, whilst the capacity was also a boon to avoid duplicates on express bookings and larger private hires.

No.87 (504 EBL) is seen against a background with much evidence of industrial archaeology in an unknown location, which compares it with what only a short time before was regarded as a typical full-size coach of the SB-series. The body on the VAL was designated 'Vega Major' in line with previous model names, but some VALs were bodied by other coachbuilders, the well-known example from the film 'The Italian Job' having a Harrington body, so was a bit of a rarity, and even a few had bus bodies.

Reliance followed the lead of Smith's, as the contracts to AERE and AWRE grew, buying some cheap used Duple-bodied Bedfords from the *George Ewer Group* and other operators based in London, with **No.88 (OGT 310)** being new to *Rickards* of W2 in 1954 with an oval-grille 'Vega' body on SBG-type chassis. Very little expense was used on these vehicles, which went onto such duties with minimum of painting, this one in August 1963, retained until 1967.

No.89 (SKR 443) was one of several nicer coaches added alongside those for just contract work, and was a 1954 SBG fitted with a 38-seater 'Venturer MkIV' body by Plaxton, arriving in 1963. With a nice interior, it was used mainly on private hires, though by this photo by Ray Simpson it was covering a Harwell contract, and it departed the fleet in January 1967, such secondhand purchases being retained for 3 to 4 years only.

No.90 (OLU 527) was another oval-grille Duple-bodied SBG new in 1954 to *Universal Sightseeing* of SW1, catering for American tourists, so it sold coaches after only a couple of seasons. It is a virtual 'twin' for No.88, and had even been with Rickards prior to Reliance. Over at Reading, could be found members of those same batches, and in fact they would rub shoulders at Harwell on contracts, that firm having OLU 528 and OGT 309!

No.91 (MAW 44) was a March 1958 Bedford SBO-type with the 'butterfly' grille design of 'Super Vega', new to *Whittles* of Highley, so had some of its beading in colours not found on the new examples, its former livery being red and blue. This 1965 view at The Wharf is by Ray Simpson, and it was sold in 1967 to an operator over at Marlow.

In this second view of that coach by Martin Shaw from 1965, we see it at the Harwell Coach Park with Wantage displayed on the front blind, a rare use of any destination on a contract coach, though there were some 30 operators serving that site, so finding your coach must have not been easy at times. AERE also ran its own fleet of vehicles for many years, some areas having housing built specially to cater for those employed at the site, whilst others covered out-of-hours and weekend requirements not on the Reliance contracts, and even using some double-deckers.

No.92 (OEL 931) was one of 8 coaches obtained to boost the contract fleet in late 1963, and one of a quartet from Bournemouth-based operator *Shamrock & Rambler*, another well-known Continental tourer. Despite that, it was a very standard Duple 'Super Vega'-bodied Bedford SBO-type new in April 1954. Dave Wilder recalled the batch as the scruffiest coaches ever in the fleet. It went to Townsend Ferries, hence this Steve Wimbush view of it taken at Dover.

No.93 (OEL 932) had a bad smash, after which it spent some time tucked away next to the Boundary Road Garage from December 1964, evidently being cannilbalised for parts to keep similar coaches on the road.

However, one of the things which made the Reliance fleet so interesting was the use of double-deckers, and here we see No.**86 (MWL 978)** again in a view taken by Philip Wallis from March 1963 laid-over at Aldermaston, with coach **No.74 (YMO 324)** having worked there from its base at Yattendon. *Smith's* also had some former *City of Oxford* AEC 'Regents' for the same purpose, and indeed No.85 (MWL 977) had been in their fleet before passing to Reliance. The location was a café nearby to the AWRE, a popular place with the drivers from both those firms. The fine condition of the 'decker is evident in this sunny photo, though the local trees took their toll of the paint on the front dome!

No.96 (KNV 442) was a 1954 Duple 'Elizabethan'-bodied 41-seater added to the fleet in May 1964. New to *KW Services* of Daventry, it was allocated to Brightwalton and used mainly on contract duties, plus some evening and weekend private hire, a nice coach on the vacuum-braked MU3RV variant of the AEC 'Reliance' chassis. It remained in service until May 1971 then went to Morris of Swansea for school contracts work. It is seen in the lower view at Gloucester Green Bus Station in Oxford, alongside a *South Midland* Bristol MW6G, and could well have been hired to *Associated Motorways* for a relief coach run, which the firm often covered when the booked seats exceeded the scheduled service coach on that network of express services, though drivers were advised to bring an overnight case as such hires often involved several journeys before it came back to the local area!

No.97 (MHO 363) was another AEC 'Reliance but carried a scarce 43-seater body by Mann Egerton of Norwich, better known as dealers most of the time. It had influences of Weymann and Roe designs, and had been supplied new in May 1954 to *Creamline* of Bordon, coming to Newbury in 1964, having a relatively short life for its type and departing after only 5 years. It is seen at Southsea in a photo by David Gillard, its career with Reliance seeing general use, though it had quite a nice interior finish.

The Mann Egerton-bodied AEC 'Reliance' was found by Martin Shaw at Harwell in September 1965, at a time when he was living near Oxford at Farmoor, so his record of local operators from the late 1950's into the '60's has proven useful in plugging gaps in the photo coverage for Reliance and also for Smith's of Reading. The body was built at a time when many small coachbuilders were trying to tap into demand, but still not sure how to treat the underfloor-engined types.

No.98 (BBL 565B) was a brand new Bedford SB13-type fitted with a 41-seat Duple (Northern) 'Firefly' body, as a direct replacement for No.79 (453 BMO) based at Yattendon, delivered in July 1964. Its well-appointed body went well with the powerful 371 Leyland engine and 5-speed gearbox, and had been bought with the Black Mountains tour very much in mind, seeing much use on the extended tours, along with quality private hires, but finally on contracts to its withdrawal in May 1977.

No.99 (ULJ 800) was another coach from the Excelsior fleet used on high-quality touring work. The chassis was an AEC 'Reliance' MU3RA (with air-braking for Continental hills), though it had appeared on the Crossley stand at the Commercial Motor Show in 1956, that maker having passed to AEC. Note the use of another distinctive number, with 800 in the same vein as 700 earlier on. It stayed with Reliance until 1972.

No.89 (ULJ 800) was duly repainted into brown and cream and was based at Newbury, where it covered a contract and some private hire at weekends. The body was another attempt by Plaxton to use Continental styling, with the roof-lights and higher waistrail. The TV-shaped radiator grille is also something of a period touch. Seen behind it is the minibus No.72 (329 ABJ) in a photo by Ray Simpson taken at Boundary Road.

No.103 (DRX 747C) was again in the normal succession of the Duple-bodied Bedford range, being a 41-seater 'Bella Vega' on SB5-type chassis, one of a pair new in June 1965. Given the set-back entrance position, the pair of nearside front seats were very popular with trippers, but the large front windscreen meant it could get very hot there as the coach headed south into the rising sun! However, it was an ideal perch for a bus-spotter out on an excursion, with a fine view of the road ahead. The upper photo was by an unknown source, but the lower view by Ray Simpson shows the offside view of these well-proportioned coaches. The body style was ideal for the application of the livery. Both the pair were allocated to Newbury for use on hire work and excursions, duly cascaded onto contract duties. This coach went in 1978, but its twin lasted until 1981. Both had further owners and 103 did not go far as it became the transport for the Nautical College situated by the Thames at Pangbourne.

No.104 (DRX 748C) was caught in the Coach Park at Southend by the author on a holiday tour of East Anglia with his parents. The signs note that some areas were reserved for off-duty buses of the Corporation at set times, but otherwise the parking was typical for its purpose at coastal resorts, using rolled gravel and prone to water-filled depressions! Better ones were at Southsea, with a large surfaced area, and Margate where the coaches used that by Dreamland.

Another view of the same coach is by Roy Marshall at The Wharf, another regular visiting enthusiast with a liking for Reliance. It was also of course a regular stop on many express routes both north-south and east-west, so a certain number of photos exist by virtue of those comfort breaks. The Wharf itself had been the designated place for carriers and buses since the Council concluded it needed to provide an area due to crowding of the Market Place in the 1920's.

No.105 (REL 55) was another refugee from Bournemouth, being new in 1955 to *Shamrock & Rambler*, coming to Newbury in 1965, mostly for contract work, though as it seated 38 it saw some use on private hires when that capacity suited. It was a Leyland-engined SB8-type Bedford with Duple 'Super Vega' body, shown after re-painting from the cream and orange livery it arrived in. It was sold to dealer Baker of Farnham in 1966 and had further owners.

(MO 6744) was a Ford 14-seat 'Tonbus' of *Freddie Spanswick*, very similar to an early *Hedge's* vehicle, with body by Andrews of Newbury, and seen here with driver George Amor, who over the years worked for many local firms and was a coachbuilder himself, so took that role in *Newbury & District* on the maintenance side when not engaged on driving duties. *Spanswick* was based at Thatcham, another carrier who followed the pattern of taking more passengers once he became motorised.

George is seen again when driving for *Andrews* of Northcroft Lane, **(BL 6490)** being one of Percy Andrews conversions from a large Talbot car bodied by that family as a 14-seater charabanc. When the author visited George at his home in Speen many years later, he produced a number of photos from his sideboard, being with *N&D* from its formation in 1932 through to the takeover by *Thames Valley* in 1950.

After the earlier carriers van and bus-types came a couple of more luxurious little 'sunsaloon' coaches on Ford AA-type chassis, and the second **(RX 6888)** is shown parked on the shingle beach at Southsea. Its body was by Duple, and proved to be a good investment, passing in and back from N&D in due course, so when it returned to Brightwalton it still bore the brown and cream livery as seen here. The early trips to the coast by Reliance would often be the first time many went to the seaside!

49

(GL 2386) was a Commer 'Centaur' with Duple coach body seating 20 bought from a Bath operator in 1937 when 2 years old, and gave 8 years good service, that make selling well at the time, with other examples locally. Seen at The Wharf, it was on the bus service in this photo alongside one of the many Thornycroft A-type buses in the *Newbury & District* fleet throughout the 1930's, ideally suited to the local roads. Note also the roof-mounted advert boards, not that common on single-deck buses, but a regular feature with N&D.

George Hedges continued to build up his local coach business after splitting from N&D, with several more secondhand additions and local takeovers to add more licensed destinations to the excursion portfolio. No.4 (VD 488) was a 1931 Gilford 168OT-type with a 32-seater Wycombe-built body, which came to him after service in Scotland and would remain in use until 1945, seen here with the wartime headlamp masks at The Wharf.

In another wartime photo by John Parke we see another Gilford, No.2 (MY 3462), a normal-control 168SD-type, by then carrying the mid-1930's 26-seater Heaver body taken off the GMC No.10 (MW 2985), whose fleet number it then assumed, running through to late 1949, by which time that once popular type was quite a rarity. It had been new in 1930 to express operator *Skylark* of London W3, one of many in that fleet.

No.39 (DLU 92) was the first double-decker in the fleet in order to meet seating requirements on contracts to AWRE at its Aldermaston site, following the lead by *Smith's* of Reading in using former *London Transport* buses, an AEC 'Regent' 0661-type of the STL class carrying a 56-seat Chiswick-built body new in 1937 and acquired in 1955. Remarkably, this bus has since survived to be fully restored at the London Transport Collection based at Brooklands, but this photo by Alan Cross caught it in its heyday of London service, complete with period adverts.

No.85 (MWL 972) also went with the trend at Smith's by next taking buses from the *City of Oxford* fleet, which had a good reputation for sound maintenance. It was also an AEC 'Regent' 0661-type with 7,7-litre oil engine new in July 1948 and carrying a 56-seater body by Weymann of Addlestone caught by the camera of Philip Wallis in 1964 at the popular Reg's Café at Tadley, a regular truck-stop and contract bus layover for the AWRE site. Note the Ford Thames and Dodge lorries also in this view.

This view of its 'twin' **No.86 (MWL 978)** is also by Philip and from 1964, but this time up at Harwell, both of those buses running on contracts for many years until replaced by 'Regent MkV's' in due course - also in parallel to events in the *Smith's* of Reading fleet. Bote the rear door added to both in due course.

No.86 (MWL 978) was of the highbridge type, the front domes of which were subjected to quite a lot of wear from the local tree-lined roads, but otherwise looks in fine shape in this view at the large bus-parking area at AWRE Aldermaston, which was established on a former USAAF airfield base, also served by its own railway station. Some 40 or so buses and coaches would be there each afternoon for the journeys covering a wide local area and operators.

No.52 (JVK 633) was one of the next AEC 'Regents' to be obtained through dealers, being a 1946 0661-type with Weymann 56-seater body new to *Northern General*. It came south in December 1957 and stayed until July 1962, being based at Newbury for use on the Aldermaston and Harwell contracts, but sometimes rarely seen on service reliefs, and was in due course repainted into full livery, though shown here still in red and cream.

The *Glasgow CT* fleet also provided a number of 'deckers for Reliance, and **No.57 (BUS 168)** was one of those, a 1938 AEC 'Regent' 0661-type, by then carrying a 1950 56-seater body built by Scottish Aviation, one of a number of aircraft builders turning to coachwork in post-war years, at a time of the re-bodying programme for that operator. It is recalled as the best of all the double-deckers, based at Newbury for the AERE/AWRE contracts, but also used on service.

The Mill Lane Shed came with the takeover of the Newbury-based business of *Enterprise Coaches*, itself started by some former *N&D* employees, giving Reliance a base in the town in an area already with many local transport connections. Indeed, that road had the former *Thames Valley* Dormy Shed, the new *N&D* Garage from the *Red & White* era, along with *Durnford & Sons* old yard used for their haulage and charabanc business. It remained in use until the opening of the Boundary Road Garage, becoming the new location for the timber yard of Travis & Arnold.

By 1966 the allocation at Newbury had outgrown the Mill Lane shed and yard, so a new garage was built around the corner in **Boundary Road,** after which the main body of the fleet was kept there, along with the maintenance area, being completed in 1963. It also incorporated office facilities, as shown to the right of this view by Ray Simpson.

A lorry or two featured in the fleet most years, and a coach was adapted for towing, but this impressive **AEC six-wheeler** was the order of the day for breakdowns in later years. Nicely painted and sign-written, it is seen by the side of the Boundary Road Garage in a photo by Ray Simpson, running on Trade Plates. However, the fleet enjoyed a good reputation for reliability, but at least the firm was prepared for any towing it might require even of sound vehicles.

No.66 (BGA 19) was one of a trio of former *Glasgow CT* AEC 'Regent' 0661-types obtained in 1959, although only 2 entered service on the Aldermaston contracts from Newbury. This 56-seater was new in October 1937 with a Cowieson body, but had been re-bodied in 1950 by Alexanders. It continued in use at Newbury until 1965, when it was replaced by a former *City of Oxford* bus of similar capacity and type. Philip Wallis saw it in 1963, by which time it was fitted with a platform door.

This 1960 view of the same bus is by Thomas W.W. Knowles confirms that the 'Private' display in the front screen was a permanent feature of those used on the contracts. Behind the bus is the Ambulance Station, backing onto the canal, whilst to the right is the one actual *Thames Valley* bus stop and shelter, a feature which went back to a wooden structure put there in the mid-1920's.

No.78 (DCK 219) bucked the trend for double-deckers in the fleet, apart from just its appearance. It was a Leyland 'Titan' PD2/3-type, and also the only lowbridge example in the fleet. New in 1951 to *Ribble Motor Services*, it was one of its 'White Lady' class of double-deck coach seating only 49, used on its express coach services, the East Lancs body having various operator features. Used mainly on the Aldermaston contracts from Newbury, it did some private hire occasionally.

No.81 (HXB 457) is one of a relatively small number of colour views of the Reliance fleet of earlier periods, despite many years of searching for them! A bit of a pity, given the nice livery and fine order of that fleet. However, Paul White was a regular visitor to his relatives in the area, so unearthed some from his old slides. This AEC 'Regal' with Duple A-type 35-seater body was new in 1946 but heavily rebuilt by the Company prior to use, only actually being sold due to the layout being by then so outdated by late 1967.

In another view of the same coach by Philip Wallis at The Wharf in March 1963, we see it awaiting a service journey, though most often to be found on contract duties, In common with many coach bodies built in the early post-war years, it arrived at Reliance showing issues caused by soft timber, so was completely rebuilt, whilst also receiving a mechanical overhaul, aided by the extensive collection of spare parts for that type.

No.60 (SME 84) was also an AEC 'Regal', though not particularly apparent in this view, with only an AEC roundel on the upper wings motif to indicate that! New in 1949, it had received this Duple body in 1954 and came to Reliance in 1958 for a stay of some 7 years, allocated to Brightwalton for use on the Cold Ash route and some private hire, shown in a Philip Wallis photo at The Wharf in July 1963. Note the touring coaches in the background.

No.54 (HYP 722) was also found by Philip Wallis that same July day, a 1948 Bedford OB with Duple 'Vista' 29-seater body with strangely red bonnet sides and mudguards at the front, probably only a stage in a repair? It had come to Reliance in 1957 and spent some time allocated to the Yattendon outstation, so used mainly on excursions and hires from that location until being transferring to the Newbury allocation in the early 1960's for contract duties until 1965.

No.76 (OLD 142) was one of several mid-capacity Bedford SB-series obtained in 1961/2, seating just 36 in its Harrington body. New in 1954 to the George Ewer Group, it first ran as Grey-Green, then later as Orange Luxury, remaining at Reliance until 1967 and used mainly on contracts, but also some private hire out of Newbury as it had a nice interior finish and was a reliable vehicle. The large front destination apertures were typical of its original owner, which operated many express services.

No 87 (504 EBL) was for many years pride-of-the-fleet from its arrival in June 1963, one of the earliest Bedford VAL-type 36-footers delivered in the Southern Counties. The Duple 'Vega Major' body had seats for 52, whilst the design permitted a virtually level floor throughout. When finally withdrawn by Reliance it was placed in store until being donated to The Science Museum, though remaining without attention ever since,

No.34 (JRX 867) was the first of the trio of the AEC 'Reliances' with 'Seagull'-style bodies by Burlingham delivered new to the firm, though some other varieties would be duly added with a variety of body types. As new these coaches were used almost continually on the coastal expresses and top-notch private hire, but in their long careers they did all end up on contracts, reliable and comfortable to the end, this example running from 1954 to 1971, a design icon of that era.

No.36 (LBL 197) was the second purchase of that type, new in 1955, worked hard on a daily basis, often to Southsea and back, where it is seen. However, when quite new it had a bad smash with an Army lorry on route for Weymouth, so returned to Burlingham to be rebuilt with a centre-doorway layout in place of that at the front as delivered. The Reliance livery well suited the lines of these coaches, which gave very reliable service for many years.

No.129 (URO 915E) had been new in July 1967 to *Fox Coaches* of Hayes and came to Newbury in September 1969. It was another Bedford VAM5-type carrying a Plaxton 'Panorama' body seating 45, used mainly on contracts, but also some private hire or excursions, staying for 10 years, another coach sold to a Welsh operator, *Bowers* of Bridgend. Where and when this photo was taken is not recorded on the print, but might be at Weymouth?

No.75 (NUY 331) was an SBO-type Bedford new in December 1956 to Tetbury Wells operator *Yarranton,* coming to Reliance in August 1961, remaining in service until the end of bus operations in the Summer of 1966. On arrival it went onto the Cold Ash route, which remained crew-operated, but later could also be found on the other services. and was the only one with moquette-covered bus seating, caught by Philip Wallis in July 1963.

No.82 (SX 8902) was one of the pair obtained after use as staff buses by *Scottish Oils*, so were not entirely PSV-compliant as received, having required some attention prior to entering service in late 1962. It is seen on the Cold Ash stand, though this bus was largely kept in reserve at Boundary Road as cover for any breakdowns of the other similar buses, also seeing use as a relief at peak times – on busy Saturday afternoons several reliefs were often needed to Cold Ash and Brightwalton!

No.80 (SX 8901) was almost exclusively to be found on the Cold Ash service, and with its high-ratio rear axle was a notably fast machine! That route had been started by *Albert Austin* before the Great War, but he returned and continued with some difficulty due to his injuries until his widow sold the service to Alan Hedges, after which it, and his excursions, were absorbed into Reliance, consolidation in that area for the firm.

The only photo of the fleet to emanate from Mike Sutcliffe was this view no doubt snapped on a layover at The Wharf, but it gives a nice snapshot of the fleet on excursions, with **No.108 (XBK 40)** and **No.103 (DRX 747C)** loading opposite the Company office. The older coach came in 1961, but the other was one of a pair new in June 1965, also illustrating how the Duple coachwork had developed in those years. Both seated 41, but the 'Bella Vega' always felt more spacious due to the extensive glazing and squarer design.

No.104 (DRX 748C) was the other of the 1965 pair, mounted on the SB5-type chassis, and both lasted in service until 1978 and 1981, earning their outlay many times over, initially on quality work and later on contracts, this one becoming transport for a dance troupe up in Shropshire after sale.

No.103 (DRX 747C) also found a non-PSV role, but nearer by at Pangbourne Nautical College when sold. However, this view by Roy Marshall at Newbury Garage shows it in its prime. The post-war contracts were the key to the continued Reliance success, and great skill was used to work those to the best economical effect, whilst also fitting in other duties such as private hires. The programme of excursions fitted in well with term-time education contracts, whilst in due course longer tours kept the firm financially sound.

No.62 (BGA 9) is seen at Aldermaston, the site being one of the largest employers in the area, with *Smith's* of Reading alone accounting for over 800 passengers on contracts to there daily! Reliance used a pair of double-deckers from Newbury for some time, whilst other routes served outlying villages over a wide area, with similar scale of operations northwards to AERE at Harwell. The AEC 7-7-litre engine was a widespread unit in the Reliance fleet.

The *Glasgow* pair at Newbury were duly replaced by a *City of Oxford* pair of 'Regent' 0661-types, of which **No.85 (MWL 972)** is seen at The Wharf on a service run, also proving that these primarily contract buses <u>did</u> have more on their blinds than just RELIANCE and PRIVATE! Both of the pair gained a rear platform door at some point, appreciated by passengers and the lady conductors on the breezy Berkshire Downs!

No.78 (DCK 219) was another stalwart of the runs to Aldermaston from Newbury, but did get to stretch its legs occasionally on some private hire, with its quite luxurious interior. Vic Norton caught it on Mill Lane in Newbury, as it passed by where the Durnford family had lived back in the 1930's, Newbury's pioneers of motor charabanc operation, as well as haulage and removals. This vehicle later joined batchmates with the Cambridge-based *Premier Travel* and still exists!

No.155 (TWR 771M) had a 45-seater 'Elite' body by Plaxton on a Bedford YRQ-type chassis, purchased in 1977 from *Perkins* over at Woodley, when about 3 years old. Note the variation in livery style, in line with trends of that period, but the lettering is an improvement after a spell where fleetnames had all but ceased to be used. It was sold in 1985 and went to Lent Rise School near Slough. This was one of many photos of the modern-era fleet taken by Phil Moth.

No.173 (TJH 881Y) shows another version of the livery experiments, having come into the fleet in April 1983, again with more prominence to the identity in this view by the coast. It was on the 11-metre Bedford YNT-type chassis, with a 53-seater 'Paramount'-style body by Plaxtons, sold in December 1985 to have a number of subsequent PSV owners. Despite the use of an out-of-area registration, it had been delivered new in 1983.

No.162 (ERX 251V) was new in May 1980, when stripes were the order of the day, okay if done well, but some liveries resembled candy bars than coaches! It was based on a Ford R1114 chassis and carried a Plaxton 'Supreme MkIII' body with seats for 53, the ultimate development in the 'Panorama' range over a number of years, offering comfort that the 1950's passenger could never have even dreamed of! The clean lines also made keeping them clean much easier.

No.165 (KBL 251W) is from the final phase of the Reliance fleet, both in its specification and the application of the revised livery. The Duple body is the 'Dominant MkIII' intended for touring work, seating 53 with plenty of luggage storage, a far cry from the 'Vista'-bodied 29-seaters of early post-war days. It was new in April 1981 on an 8.25-litre Bedford YNT chassis, seen at the British Coach Rally on Madeira Drive on Brighton's sea front.

Also by the sea, but this time on the Island of Gozo, is former Reliance **No.170 (LVS 435V)**, one of 13 coaches from the fleet to be exported to the Maltese Islands. It was a Bedford YMT with Plaxton 53-seater 'Supreme MkIV' body, which passed to *Charles Borg* of Doraui and was caught by Mac Head on one of his visits to the resort, when he sought out those coaches, which ended up either on tourist work, or on the bus route network.

Seen bearing Flight's Travel names is former Reliance **No. 174 (LTF 224P)** with *Joseph Grima* of Qala, the grey and red scheme being the usual for vehicles on Gozo. Some of those on Malta ran in a green livery at first, but the more familiar yellow and orange replaced that. All were re-registered, several times in some cases, so some detective work was required to unravel their previous identities. Even the Reliance Director Gordon Hedges took a trip to try to locate them!

Former **No.142 (UJB 726N)** is seen in the familiar 'sunshine' livery usually associated with Malta buses, though all were individually operated, so variety had been evident in earlier times. It went to Marco Mallia of Santa Venera and gained a new guise as DBY 343, but quite why the Buckingham name was added is not known. It was on express bus duties when caught at Valetta's busy Bus Station, hub of the main island's services around the central fountain, still looking in fine condition.

Former No.153 (OAN 963R) basks in the sun on a layover, the stalls typical of the Bus Station area, and behind it appears to be an ex-London AEC 'Swift', though all vehicles were modified by their new owners to some extent, the descriptions sometimes being relevant, as with this Duple 'Dominant'-style coach, as well as the Bedford engine designation shown on the side panel.

Again, with relevant badges adorning it we see former **No.147 (HGM 822M)** in Valetta Bus Station, with some older types still evident to the rear. Malta was once a haven for finding old buses and coaches, many hiding their true identities well, some even based on old Army lorries abandoned during the War, all now swept away by newer types and regulations, but maybe in a barn somewhere lurks one still with an ancestry in West Berkshire waiting one day to be repatriated?!

On Instructions of Reliance Motor Services (Newbury) Ltd. due to cessation of business

On Site at the Coach Station, Boundary Road, Newbury, Berkshire

Dispersal Sale of the Complete

WORKSHOP TOOLS
and EQUIPMENT
SPARE PARTS, etc.

including

TRANSMISSION & BOTTLE JACKS • WORKSHOP
LATHES • DRILLS • WELDERS • WASHERS
GRINDERS • POLISHERS • COMPRESSORS
ELECTRICAL & AIR TOOLS • TESTING EQUIPMENT
& PRECISION TOOLS • BEDFORD Y & FORD R SERIES
SPARES • ENGINES • SPRINGS & SHACKLES
WHEELS & TYRES • ELECTRICAL • OFFICE
EQUIPMENT AND NUMEROUS MISCELLANEOUS
ITEMS • IN ALL SOME 800 LOTS

FOR SALE BY AUCTION

**TUESDAY, 8th APRIL, 1986
at 10.00 a.m.**

Auctioneers

Thimbleby & Shorland

Reading

No.108 (XBK 40) was an SB1-type Bedford with 41-seater Duple 'Super Vega' body acquired September 1965, but new to *Byng's* of Southsea, so often to be seen at that location as in this view. It had come via *Stout's* of Shalbourne, also long-established Carriers to Newbury from the 1920's. David Gillard took a few photos of the Reliance fleet and sent them to the author in response to his appeal. It spent time on mixed duties until sold in 1974 to *House* of Hilton for further use.

No.109 (KCP 725) was one of a number of secondhand purchases in 1965-6, used mainly on contracts, though those with better interiors saw more private hire work. Seen at Southsea in a Ray Simpson photo, it carried a 41-seater Plaxton 'Consort' body, new 1959 in Halifax to *Anderson*, but reached Newbury via Marlborough-based *Prout* in March 1966, staying for 6 years before moving to a Welsh owner. As well as generally making side windows larger on its body designs, Plaxton experimented with larger windscreens, though drivers complained of the reflections from passing vehicles.

In the lower view of the same coach by the author, we see the offside, along with the style of front panel and, whilst this view also accords us a look at the rear-end layout of the rarer Mann Egerton body on AEC 'Reliance' **No.97 (MHO 363)**, a quite plain but neat profile, complete with the typical Reliance signwriting of the period.

No.110 (GRX 398D) was half of the new intake for the 1966 season, both being 45-seater 'Bella Venture' Duple-bodied Bedford VAM5-type chassis and new in March. It is shown on a coastal excursion or an express, their prime duties when new, though both were duly cascaded to take advantage of the higher capacity on contracts. Both it and twin No.111 (GRX 399D) passed to an old customer *Henderson* of Penycraig when sold in 1980.

No.111 (GRX 399D) was caught by the author on one of his many trips to the races on the coaches of *Gough's Garage* of Bracknell, where his Father's fellow employees as coach drivers always made him welcome. In the background we have a tour coach from the *Souhdown* fleet, with a *Ribble* day-trip on the right, both of those being on Leyland 'Leopard' chassis, with Harrington and Plaxton bodies, so a good snapshot of that era.

No.111 (GRX 399) shows how the VAM allowed its maker to at last offer a type suitable for a true front-entrance body, the point having been proven after the coachbuilder Yeates had produced an SB variant converted by re-positioning the front axle, though no examples ran for Reliance. However, the VAM was not a match for heavier chassis types, so when *Thames Valley* ordered a quartet for the Reading to Heathrow Rail-Air service, the Bedford rep was apparently rather shocked!

No.113 (WLB 420) was another of the 1966 intake, being a 1959 SB3-type with 41-seater 'Super Vega' body, originating in Enfield with *Alexandra Coaches*. It was used mainly on contracts and is seen waiting the afternoon run from Harwell, though to quite where is not shown, but some of the *Smith's* drivers would put seaside places on the blind to cheer up the workers! This coach was converted to SB1 type before use and was sold off in September 1974, always a change-over time of year for education contracts.

No.114 (4590 NA) also was converted to the SB1 specification prior to service, another SB3 when new in March 1960 to *Spencer Tours* in Manchester, with similar body to the one above. This arrived in late 1966 and was based at the Brightwalton Garage, being used on contracts on weekdays, but seeing some excursions and private hire at other times through to its disposal in February 1973.

No.115 (6706 WE) was another from the North, new in March 1959 to *Hirst & Sweeting* of Sheffield, but with a 41-seater Plaxton 'Consort MkIV' body, over to Reliance in 1967 mainly for contract duties. As with other coaches obtained at that time it ran in a cream livery, never gaining brown paint or fleetnames, always intended for lesser duties, though at times seeing some private hire for schools, a lot of which fitted in nicely with contract obligations to complete a working day.

No.115 (6706 WE) One of the highlights of the calendar was the Commercial Motor Show, then held annually, where new chassis types and body designs were unveiled, and the author was fortunate that his Father was invited to attend through his Motor Trade contacts. By then the UK coach body market was dominated by Duple and Plaxton, vying with each other for both the front- and underfloor-engine chassis ranges, with many orders taken during the Show.

No.116 (XOU 377) was also the same coachwork on a Bedford SB1-type chassis, new in May 1960 to *Marchwood Motorways* of Totton, acquired in 1966/7. After its withdrawal during September 1974, it was another member of the fleet to find a new home with a operator in Wales, many of the sales both in and out of the fleet then being through the Farnham-based Bakers dealership, where a good selection of used vehicles could always be found.

No.117 (AMC 351A) was one of 4 vehicles acquired with the business of *Cooper* of Upper Bucklebury in early 1967, a small but well-kept outfit which traded as *Ivory Coaches* from its base at Cooper's Garage. It was one of a pair new to *Frames Tours* of London in November 1965, Bedford SB8-types with Plaxton 'Embassy Mk11 bodies seating 41, that style featuring a peaked front dome, much neater than the other examples on this page.

No.118 (AMC 352A) looks as good as new in this view at The Wharf, hired in by *Associated Motorways* to help out on an express working to Worthing. Most of the time though, this pair from *Cooper* were mainly to be found on local private hires and covering excursions as also taken over from that location, a useful extension to established holdings, all part of the ongoing process of Reliance expansion which made it the premier operator for the area.

No.119 (200 GMY) also hailed from the Bucklebury takeover, being a 1958 AEC 'Reliance' MU3RV-type and carrying a front-entrance 'Britannia' body by Duple, but only seating 30 in a 2+1 arrangement, also new to *Frames Tours*. Despite that apparent oddity, it was based at the Brightwalton Garage and was used mostly on contracts through to 1971 when sold to Swansea-based *Morris*.

No.121 (KMD 440C) was a Bedford SB5 new to *Martin* of West End, near Bagshot, in 1965, coming to Newbury some 3 years later. With its 41-seater 'Bella Vega' style body, it was mainly used on private hire and excursions, later cascaded onto contract runs and lasting until March 1981. It is shown in Bath, an ever-popular destination for coach trips, and also used as a lunch stop on the tours to the West Country, caught by the author on one of his regular visits to that interesting place.

No.122 (600 DBU) was another 'Embassy MkII' 41-seater body on Bedford chassis, new in April 1963 to *Don's* of Southsea, coming to Reliance 5 years later for mainly contract duties, seen here in this Thomas Knowles photo at Harwell with No.113 (WLB 420). Some of its 10-year stay in the fleet saw it based at Yattendon, where it replaced No.74 (YMO 324) as the local allocation, where it enjoyed some more varied work away from the pattern of daily contract runs.

No.123 (7467 FH) was not actually the next minibus in the fleet, as *Cooper* had contributed No.120 (CBL 488B), though that seems somewhat camera-shy compared with this Commer 1500LBD-type with its Harrington-built 12-seater body, shown in the area usually associated with excursion departures at The Wharf, with the offices, shops and cafes of The Old Ganary to its rear. It had been new in 1974 to *Tomlinson* of Fairford.

No.124 (5900 EL) was one of a number of coaches emanating from the touring fleet of *Shamrock & Rambler* of Bournemouth, though out of a trio bought in early 1968, only this one entered service. New in May 1960, it was an SB1-type carrying a Harrington 'Crusader' 41-seater body. As it was, when 7402/3 EL were checked over, the work needed on them meant they never became part of the active fleet, but were a source of spare parts.

No.124 (5900 EL) is shown again in another Ray Simpson view at Boundary Road. The body style used by the Hove-based factory never worker as well on front-engine types as for the underfloor-engine chassis, with their front domes and over-hang. The unusual name of the operator had been derived by the coming together of two charabancs operators from the early days, but in later times the firm had concentrated on high-class touring in the UK and on the Continent.

No.125 (ROD 767) was part of the final generation of double-deckers at Reliance, which followed the trend set by *Smith's* of Reading once again in its choice. This MCCW-bodied 59-seater carried the 'Orion'-style body on an AEC 'Regent MkV' chassis, so it was mechanically similar to the 'Reliances' in the fleet. It had been new in 1956 to *Devon General*, one of a 'pair' bought to replace older 'Regents' Nos.85/6 (MWL 972/8) on Aldermaston runs from Newbury.

No.125 (ROD 767) is seen again in company with its 'twin' **No.126 (TTT 781)** of the same type and origins, having the AEC A170 vertically-mounted engine, which the fitters already new well in its horizontal guise as part of the coach fleet. Both were acquired in August 1968. The dark red of their former owner was retained, neither ever being re-painted into the full brown and cream scheme.

No.126 (TTT 781) had been new in June 1959, and this nesarside view by Graham Low shows the lack of bead lines on that body design, quoted by *Smith's* of Reading as to why it did not paint the similar examples it had from the *South Wales* and *Rhondda* fleets into its distinctive orange and blue livery, perhaps the same occurring at Reliance? Both of these 'Regent MkV's did, in course, contribute in some way to the preservation of that type.

No. 128 (RHK 701D) was a good coach very similar to No.121, being a Bedford SB5 with Duple 'Bella Vega' 41-seater body, new in June 1966 to *Tiffin* of Brentwood, coming to Newbury 3 years later for general coaching duties before ending up on contract runs. Seen here alongside 1962 No.79 (453 BMO) it shows how the Duple coachwork of that period had evolved. When sold it went to *Tally Ho* of Kingsbridge in South Devon.

No.127 (VBL 413G) was a Ford R226 chassis fitted with a 52-seater 'Panorama Elite'-style body by Plaxton and purchased new in June 1969. Its fine interior can be seen through the large side windows when caught at Gloucester Green in Oxford, touring work then becoming more of a feature by the Company. Martin Shaw took the photo, another enthusiast kindly donating his pictures, whilst the coach remained with Reliance until May 1982. So was a good buy.

No.129 (URO 915E) was a secondhand Bedford VAM5-type carrying a 45-seater Plaxton 'Panorama' body, new in 1967 to *Fox* of Hayes, coming to Newbury in September 1969. By then the Bus Station had moved from The Wharf to Market Street, on a site close by the Mayors Lane former garage of *Durnford & Sons,* on the left of this view. In the background lurks one of those odious 'Nationals' by Leyland, operating for the successor of *Thames Valley* in whatever name it was at that time. This coach was sold in 1979.

No.132 (FGF 474C) was a further 'Bella Vega'-bodied Bedford but of the SB13 variety with Leyland 0.370 oil engine, new in June 1965 to *Hall's* of Hounslow, coming west to Newbury in 1971 for a 5-year stay, used widely on most coaching duties, and caught here by the camera of Brian Botley at Southsea, one of a few from the fleet there on that day. The same coach was also seen by Philip Wallis at The Wharf on 26th November 1971, either on an excursion or private hire. The Wharf was quite a hub of express coach services, both north-to-south and east-to-west at that time, bringing many far-flung coaches from the Associated Motorways partners, as well as hired-in ones, whilst Newbury was also a convenient lunch stop om many touring itineries, so there was always something else to see alongside the daily *Thames Valley* and Reliance fleets. A *Royal Blue* Bristol RELH6G attracts attention.

No.131 (XMO 455H) was the only full-size coach bought in 1970, delivered in May with a 52-seater Plaxton 'Panorama Elite' body on another Ford R226-type chassis, marking the re-emergence of Ford as a dedicated builder of PSV chassis after many years out of that market, an event quite unexpected at the time. They proved an economical choice, no doubt encouraging Bedford to develop its successful Y-series to replace the less-than-great VAM-types, as we shall see in due course.

The same coach is shown at the Boundary Road Garage, where the dedicated maintenance team was headed by the Directors, to ensure that the Reliance fleet was always smartly turned out, all without the aid of a mechanised washer! The author recalls now the horror of the day he heard that Reliance was to end, it just did not seem to be possible, though the odd rumour of the firm being up for possible sale had already reached his ears.

No.135 (EAD 361C) was yet another 'Bella Vega' 41-seater on Bedford chassis added secondhand for contract work in 1971, being some 6 years old then, and new to *Talbot* of Moreton. Thast style of body was notably more spacious than others of the same capacity, so they made good general coaches. It is seen here at Winchester Coach Station in a photo by Thomas W.W. Knowles – note the bar and the weighing scales in the background at that location.

No.134 (CWH 788C) had also been new in 1965 to the Bolton-based operator *Leigh,* carrying a 'Panorama'-style Plaxton body with seats for 41. It came to Newbury in 1971 for the usual mix of weekday contracts, plus some evening and weekend excursions and private hires through to withdrawal in 1976 and sale to *Allan* of Stamford Bridge. Ray Simpson found it outside the Newbury Garage with one of the more exotically-bodied former *Excelsior* coaches in the background.

No.138 (ODD 166F) also bore a 'Panorama' 41-seater body on a Bedford SB5 chassis, new to Talbot of Moreton-in-Marsh in June 1968, passing to the firm in October 1972. Seen here in a Thomas Knowles' photo standing between 'Firefly'-bodied No.98 (BBL 665B) and No.132 (FGF 474C) with 'Bella Vega' bodywork, showing some of the variety then on offer in the fleet. It was used mainly on contracts, being withdrawn in August 1982, when it was sold to *Shiel* of Archaracle

In this offside view of the same coach in a rural setting, we can see how the 'Panorama' style was developing, with its notably large side windows and wrap-round windscreen. The Harwell contracts went far out to encompass most of the villages of West Berksahire, along with the adjoining areas in Wiltshire and Oxfordshire, whilst those to Aldermaston also ran in from Hampshire.

No.135 (EAD 361C) is seen in another photo by Thomas W.W. Knowles at the Boundary Road Garage, as a younger member of the family is receiving instruction on coach-washing the traditional way. It was indeed rare to see a dirty Reliance coach, whilst any odd scrapes or knocks were generally dealt with by the Night Foreman and often blamed on the garage cat! The purchase of sound secondhand stock usually resulted in about 5 years of trouble-free service for minimum outlay.

No.136 (DJH 733F) was the only example of the Duple 'Viceroy' body in the fleet, on a Bedford VAM70-type chassis with Leyland 4.66-litre oil engine. It had been new to *Spence* of High Wycombe in June 1968 and came to Reliance in April 1971 to put in 9 years of use. Note the Ice Cream Kiosk, then a staple of any coach park at the time, along with those dispensing tea, crisps and chocolate - no 98 varieties of coffee to contend with!

No 139 (FUP 572H) is seen at Bourton-on-the-Water in a photo by the author on a regular family trip there, his sister particularly liking paddling in the little stream which runs through it, a popular day-trip with generations, with its various attractions including the Motor Museum. It is also the base for *Pulham's Coaches* a 1920's carrier-cum-coach operator, paralleling similar development to Reliance, even including local bus operations.

No.140 (DJH 750G) was also a Bedford VAM70 new in March 1969 to *Hanworth Acorn* of Bedfont, coming via *Reed* of Holyport to the fleet in late 1972. It carried a 45-seater 'Panorama Elite' body and Phil Moth found it at Royal Ascot Races one June, parked between other Plaxton-bodied coaches. It duly went to *Henderson* of Penyraig, the second most popular destination for sold Reliance coaches after the Maltese Islands!

In the offside view of that coach by Thomas Knowles, it is seen on a theatre outing to Stratford-upon-Avon, the development of the 'Panorama' style now doing away with any opening side windows, though as the roof vents are all open, it must have been quite a warm day, or perhaps the driver found it too hot to sleep, long hours often being worked from preparing the coach in the morning through to putting it away after the day's trip.

No.133 (BSY 418C) was a 1965 Bedford SB5 with 41-seater 'Bella Vega' body, bought in 1971 primarily for weekday contract duties, though when found by the author in a side-street in Marlborough nearby the Kennet & Avon Canal it was on a private hire for a school party. When it was withdrawn in 1982 it was used to keep similar vehicles on the road, and it is worth mentioning that Marlborough College was a regular hirer of coaches from the firm, whilst there were runs from that area to Harwell for its workers.

We now come to a selection of views of groups of vehicles, the first two from a visit to Newbury in passing by Ken Jubb which lay forgotten for many years until the author put an appeal through the PHRG of the Omnibus Society for this album. To the right of his panoramic sweep we see AEC 'Regal' **No.63 (LPA 952)**, AEC 'Regent' **No.62 (BGA 9)** and Bedford OB No**. 23 (ERX 284)**, whilst on the left-hand portion next we have AEC 'Regent' **No.52 (JVK 633)**, and 'Regals **No. 28 (HON 623)** and **No.63** again. These were part of the Newbury allocation in the Mill Lane yard prior to the opening of Boundary Road Garage, the new fuel tanks also just visible on the kerb awaiting installation at that site. These photos were another example of a young enthusiast who happened to pass through Newbury on a longer journey that day, the independent being a fleet worth a second look and taking some photos.

With the opening of the Boundary Road Garage most of the fleet became based there, with less then at Brightwalton, and a few at places such as Yattendon. This view of that garage shows, left to right, **Nos 143 (UJB 727N), 173 (TJH 881Y), 165 (KBL 251W, 162 (ERX 251V)** and **142 (UJB 726N**), which gives a date taken of after April 1983. Note the quite industrial landscape to the rear, that area being one of various mills, including some water-powered ones associated with the nearby Kennet & Avon Canal.

Ray Simpson supplied many photos to the author in his teenage days, finding this variety at Boundary Road to show Mann Egerton-bodied AEC 'Reliance' **No.97 (MHO 363),** Bedford **No.79 (453 BMO),** AEC 'Regent MkV' **No.126 (TTT 781)** and Plaxton-bodied Bedford **No.116 (XOU 377),** which means it must be taken between 1968 and 1974 and only *Smith's* of Reading could rival such a variety locally.

Philip Wallis managed to catch the buses on all three of the service routes one day in November 1963, with **No. 73 (NTH 690)** on Cold Ash**, No.80 (SX 8901)** on Brightwalton and **No.75 (NUY 331)** on the Wantage run. All were Duple (Midland)-bodied Bedford SB's, whilst similar bus No.82 (SX 8902) was kept in reserve if required, or did come out on a relief, as did even double-deckers at peak times!

The third line-up was by the author during a 1970 visit, by which time he was using 36-shot films in place of his earlier roll with only 8 shots! Left to right at the pumps on the frontage of Boundary Road were Bedfords **No.108 (XBK 40), No.129 (URO 915E), No.74 (YMO 324), No.104 (DRX 748C)** and **No.116 (XOU 377),** AEC 'Regent MkV' **No.125 (ROD 767)** and Bedford **No.128 (RHK 701D).** Again, the variety in types and body styles was at that time quite interesting, whilst the inclusion of 'deckers was a factor in making the fleet of interest,

Philip Wallis paid a visit to Newbury on a chilly February day in the bad Winter of 1963, catching Bedford **No.74 (YMO 324),** AEC 'Reliance' **No.67 (VMO 440)** and one of the former *City of Oxford* 'Regents' **Nos. 85 or 86 (MWL 972/8**). The author **h**ad a difficult time travelling from Bracknell to Windsor for school, the Windsor Forest area being badly affected, but nothing like it must have been over in West Berkshire, though the bus services continued and Reliance persevered!

Martin Shaw's photos of Reliance also form an important record of its fleet and operations, and here we see three classic types taken together at the Newbury Garage, a Duple 'Vista'-bodied Bedford OB, an AEC 'Regent' 'decker from City of Oxford **No. 85 (MWL 972)** and Duple 'Super Vega'-bodied Bedford **No.108 (XBK 40)**, and I am grateful to Martin for making his prints available to me when the call went out, helping to plug some gaps in this fleet and S*mith's* of Reading.

Ray Simpson continued to record the Reliance fleet into quite modern times, as did Phil Moth, and a photo by the former shows Plaxton 'Supreme'-bodied Bedford YRT-type **No.159 (LDN 513N)** and Duple 'Dominant MkIII'-bodied Ford R1114-type **No.161 (YCF 967T)** on a job together in 1979 – a newer generation of coaches, but still well-kept and a credit to all those at Reliance!

No.137 (JRL 552E) was a 1967 Bedford VAM14 with Plaxton 'Panorama MkII' 45-seater body into the fleet in February 1973 having come from *Fry of Tintagel* in Cornwall. It was used on contracts in the main, plus some excursions and hires. In this photo by Phil Moth it is in shown with a *Barnes of Aldbourne*, the only old family operator around Newbury to continue after the demise of Reliance, providing a link to Newbury on market days back to horse-drawn days, which produced its own history many years ago and worth a read, entitled 'From A Packet of Pins'.

No.144 (ULT 442M) was a further minibus to continue to provide a smaller capacity for lesser hires and lightly loaded contracts, a Ford 'Transit' long-wheelbase with 12-seater body by Bristol Street Motors, new in May 1975 and remaining until June 1985.

No.141 (UJB 725N) was one of a trio of new Bedford YRQ's fitted with Duple 'Dominant' bodies, this one with 45 seats new in August 1974. All initially on front-line duties, they were to be found on coastal expresses, excursions and private hires, all of them putting in 10 years of fine service, this being one of the coaches later exported to Malta for a new career in the sun as a local service bus dashing about that island, but seen here on a local school trip, one of the bread-and-butter tasks for Reliance over the decades, often fitting in with education contracts.

No.143 (UJB 727N) was the 53-seater of that trio with an additional window bay along its sides beyond the emergency exit door. At that time the 'Panorama' and 'Dominant' bodies by Plaxton and Duple were the mainstay of a body market then still to see the rise of foreign coachbuilders into the UK, on what were still mostly UK-built chassis types as well, but the next decade would bring a shift on both fronts, as we shall see later on.

No.145 (HGM 820N) was a Bedford SB5, a type still in production despite good order books for the Y-series, suited to this 41-seater version of the Duple 'Dominant' body, fulfilling the need for private hires not economical with larger coaches. It was caught by Thomas W.W. Knowles in the front yard at Boundary Road. New in July 1975, it went relatively early in 1982, initially to a Welsh operator, but in due course was exported to Pakistan!

No.147 (HGM 822N) came at a time of changing trends in private hires, as in earlier decades many people belonged to clubs and groups, which had organised outings, but by the 1970's a combination of private car ownership and the shift from such activities had reduced such hires, coming at a time when coach bodies had even more seats to fill, so a 'bums-on-seats' situation had affected capacity on the coastal runs and excursions as well, eroding much of the traditional income for such operators as Reliance.

No.146 (KCF 27P) was therefore another 41-seater replacement for the fleet arriving in October 1975, a Bedford SB5-type again with Duple 'Dominant' bodywork, seen in another photo by Thomas Knowles, one of the most prolific of photographers of the fleet in that period, so a special thanks to him for allowing use of his prints. Sold after 8 years, it continued in use with *Reynolds of Caister*, its career with Reliance being on general duties as befitted the body capacity.

No.149 (LTF 224P), on the other hand is an anonymous photo by someone who found it parked by the Queen Elizabeth Hall on London's South Bank complex, the site in 1951 of the Festival of Britain. It had the 53-seater 'Dominant' body mounted on a Bedford YMT chassis. It was new to Reliance in June 1976, despite its out-of-area registration, and after withdrawal in December 1985 went for a new life on the Island of Gozo, and it can be seen in that new guise on page 62.

No.150 (NMO 66R) is a Phil Moth photo, who took many of the fleet, and has also printed up many acquired negatives which help cover the modern era of that operator. This view includes an RF-type saloon, which suggests a bus rally venue, perhaps the Alton event? It was new in early 1977 as a 53-seater Duple 'Dominant'-bodied YMT-type Bedford, and was also one of the coaches later to be exported to Malta at the cessation of operations.

No.152 (OAN 962R) was one of a number of the fleet caught by Phil Moth on Derby Day at Epsom, the event being very popular in an area dominated by horse-racing interests based in Lambourn, the Ilsleys and the Marlborough Downs over the decades. It not only featured the racing but had many catering tents and a fun-fair atmosphere. New in May 1977, this was one of a pair of YRQ-type Bedfords with 'Dominant' 45-seater bodies, also later exported to Malta.

No.154 (OAN 964R) is also seen on the approach to the Coach Park at Epsom Race Course, perched high on the Downs. Loadings were good on these trips, all the local villages being added to the Road Service Licenses over the years to give Reliance an important annual income, especially after *Thames Valley* had given up offering excursions from Newbury as its fleet was reduced during the early 1960's. The excellent condition of the Reliance fleet is clear.

No.155 (TWR 771M) was a Bedford YRQ-type with a Plaxton 'Elite'-style body with 45 seats, new in June 1974 to *Anderson of Keighley* in Yorkshire, via *Perkins of Woodley* to the fleet in September 1977. It was given this experimental livery, one of several styles tried out during that period, and can be seen in full-colour on page 61. The use of stripes and go-faster lines was then replacing the traditional liveries as used on the old body types, note also the larger fleetname.

No.156 (TOT 245M) was another YRQ new in June 1974 to *Budden's Coaches* of Woodfalls in Hampshire, another long-established operator, again seen at The Derby in June, passing a bizarrely-painted ex-London 'Routemaster' bus, the event attracting all sorts of vehicles for use as grand-stands for the races. This coach came to Reliance in April 1978 and then sold for further service, as were most coaches of that era, many going to operators in Wales through dealer connections.

No.157 (KPC 213P) was a nice secondhand purchase through the Farnham-based dealer Bakers, being new in September 1975 to *Gale's of Haslemere*. It was a YRQ type Bedford with 45-seater 'Dominant' body acquired in April 1978 when the fleet was being updated without too much expenditure over new stock, the financial situation being less sound than in earlier times. A photo by Ray Simpson of Oxford, who covered the operator well over the years.

No.159 (LDN 513N) in a view by Thomas Knowles, who in recent times has been sharing his photos through the PSV Circle, the fleet being a favourite of his during his years in the area. It was a YRT-type and carried a full-size Plaxton 'Supreme' body, the first in the fleet when it came in November 1978 when just over 3 years old. When sold it did not go far, but to the Upper Heyford-based firm of *Heyfordian,* who also ran contracts into Harwell.

No.159 (LDN 513N) is seen in another Thomas Knowle's photo at the Newbury Garage forecourt, though its livery has been altered since the other view, part of experiments then in progress. The 'Supreme' body was the ultimate type in the 'Panorama' range that had started back in the early 1960's, making the Scarborough-based Plaxton the most popular builder of coach bodies in the UK at that time. They had adapted Continental features such as air-conditioning and space for passenger's luggage as the range developed.

No.158 (TWR 772M) had the 'Elite'-style body also by Plaxton, having been new in 1974 to *Cooper* based in Ecclestone up in Yorkshire, coming to the fleet in October 1978 to replace an older coach, staying until August 1985, when operations began to wind down at Reliance. It is again shown approaching the Coach Park on Derby Day, a nice neat coach, and a credit to the maintenance standards of the Boundary Road staff of the period.

No.160 (YCF 966T) marked a return to the original chassis maker used by George Hedges, being a Ford R1114-type, one of a pair new in May 1979 with Duple 'Dominant MkIII'-style 53-seater bodies. It is seen in this Thomas Knowle's photo at Newbury Garage carrying a variety of fleetname styles, another experimental topic of the period, in order to update the appearance were being considered. It went to Malta during August 1985.

No.162 (ERX 251V) was seen by Phil Sposito on a trip to Newbury Garage, receiving the traditional wash-and-brush-up given to each coach daily, there being no automated washer. By the time this one of a pair of Ford R1114's came in May 1980 the livery had settled down to as shown here, also marking a switch back to Plaxton, with the MkIII version of the 53-seater 'Supreme' body. By coincidence, both this and twin No.163 ended up as Scout transport in the area around Guildford, and each via *Barfoot* of West End.

No.165 (KBL 251W) will also be found in the colour section, as when very new it took part in the British Coach Rally at Brighton in April 1981. That 27th event of an annual nature gave the opportunity to show off the latest coaches, with competitions for driving skills as well, and was well supported by the industry, though it was the only entry for Reliance, and Phil Moth got plenty of photos on that occasion. As can be seen from the upper view the coach was well presented for the day, whilst the lower shot shows the extensive areas for luggage, now necessary for the extended tours being operated, also a good move to restore the financial position of the Company as the old ways of attracting custom had been eroded by private car use and cheaper holidays by air with the advent of package deals. The scene is Madeira Drive, where the driver did well to handle the 11-metre length during the skill tests!

No.165 (KBL 251W) also brought with it another style of livery and lettering, and the full effect can be seen on page 63 of the full colour section, also taken by Phil Moth. The longer tours involved overnight travel, something hard to contemplate in the older type coaches, whilst the high waistline and windows were ideally placed for good views without glare, the 'Dominant MkIII' body seating 53 and mounted on a Bedford YNT chassis new in the Spring of 1981.

No.168 (BPG 777T) was one of several secondhand coaches added alongside the investment in new ones, as at the time the family were in the complex process of deciding whether to continue or not. It was a YNT-type carrying a 53-seater 'Supreme MkIV' body new in March 1979 to *Bicknell* of Godalming, used by Reliance on works and school contracts, but despite such attempts to contain costs, various other factors would heap more pressures on the Directors.

No.170 (LVS 435V) was a YMT-type new in April 1980 to *Buker* of London SW6 for high-class tourist work, coming to Newbury in May 1982, the financial climate affecting many operators. It carried a 53-seat 'Supreme MkIV' body, and is seen at The Derby in a photo by Phil Moth. It duly went to the Maltese Island of Gozo, and a photo of its afterlife there can be found on page 62 in colour, being one of 13 Reliance coaches to be exported for further service to Malta.

No.172 (TJH 882Y) was a new 53-seater YNT-type with the 'Paramount' body by Plaxton, purchased in April 1983, the last-but-one batch of new vehicles for the fleet. The candy-striped livery had by then become rather dated, whilst the style of fleetname had also settled down, the overall effect now much neater. Thomas Knowles caught it at the South Coast, and after sale it remained in the UK with *Prosser* of Bratton Fleming.

No.175 (A64 YRD) was the next vehicle to cover the small-capacity role, being used for smaller private hires and contract runs, new in March 1984, being a FIAT 35.B-type fitted with a 12-seater body by Robin Hood Coach Works, but badged as an IVECO under license. The Italian maker FIAT had been a popular choice back in the 1920's, used locally by various of the carriers and chara firms, but had largely disappeared from the PSV market in Britain for many years.

No.176 (VPR 864X) was the final secondhand purchase by Reliance in August 1984, when it was just over 3 years old, YNT-type Bedford carrying a 53-seater 'Supreme MkIV' body, new to *Billie's* of Mexborough but coming via another. It was yet another attending the Derby at Epsom, all the coaches carrying stickers to show which party they were for, and also the parking area to be used, with many coaches from all over the country. It ended up as a tourist coach on the Island of Gozo.

Reliance already had an extensive range of excursions, which it had continued licenses for after the split from N&D, with additions over the years prior to WW2, all of which were renewed post war. However, of particular significance post-war were the many contract operations, along with consolidations through local takeovers for excursions and tours.

17.7.1949 - Alan Hedges takeover licenses of Albert Austin, Stage Service as Cold Ash (Bucklebury Alley) to Newbury (Wharf).

25.3.50 Former Austin E&Ts from Cold Ash to Brighton, Bournemouth, Portsmouth, Weymouth, Weston-Super-Mare, Southampton, Hayling Island and Bognor Regis, plus additions of Blenheim Palace, Swanage, Littlehampton, Hastings, Southend, Windsor & Burnham Beeches, Harringay, Highworth Speedway, Cowley Speedway, Regents Park for Festival of Britain, Blackpool Illuminations, circular tours as Lambourn. Hungerford, Kingsclere, California-in-England, Thame, Brimpton Common, Pewsey, Worcester & Malvern tour and Aldershot tattoo, some others discontinued

25.3.50 New express carriage Eastbury to AERE via Eastbury -West Shefford - Chaddleworth – Leckhampstead – Brightwalton Turn – Lilley – Farnborough – West Ilsley – Harwell.

1.3.52 - Express carriage Lambourn – AERE via Lambourn – letcombe Bassett – Letcombe Regis.

14.3.1953 - Official address now No.1 The wharf, Newbury.

15.3.53 - New express carriages to Central Ordnance depot, Didcot from Newbury via Hermitasge – Hampstead Norris – Compton - and from Newbury via Chieveley – Beedon – East Ilsley , and from West Ilsley via Est Ilsley.

25.4.53 Additional E&Ts from Brightwalton to Highcliffe, Swanage, Littlehampton, Hastings, Chessington Zoo, Worcester & Malvern tour, Silverstyone, Harringay, London Theatres, Blenheim Palace, Coronation Route, Coronation Day, Cowley and Highworth (both Speedway).

14.11.53 – New express carriage Hungerford – AWRE Aldermaston via Kintbury – Speen – Newbury – Thatcham.

17.4.54 – New express carriage from Shefford Woodlands to Aldermaston AWRE via Hungerford Newtown – Hungerford – Speen – Newbury – Thatcham.

15.5.54 - Reliance MS takes over E&Ts license of Alan Hedges from Cold Ash, and adds White City, Kew Gardens, Hampton Court, Beckkonscot & Burnham Beeches, Shakespear Country, Cirencester & Bourton-on-the-Water and Southend. Also takes over stage carriage from Cold Ash to Newbury.

27.11.54 – New express carriage from Shefford to Harwell AERE via East Garston – Eastbury – Lambourn – Wantage. Aldermaston contract to start from Ramsbury via Chilton Foliat, then Hungerford etc.

23.7.55 – Take over of E&Ts from Yattendon formerly granted to John Donovan as Portsmouth, Bournemouth, Swindon, Abingdon, Windsor, Reading, Devises, Aldershot, Tidworth, Basingstoke, Winchester, Southampton, Weymouth, Wallingford, Hungerford, Salisbury, Andover.

22.5.55 – New express carriage to AWRE Aldermaston from Ashampstead via Yattendon – Frilsham – Hermitage – Long Lane – Cold ash – Bucklebury – Woolhampton. Additional E&Ts from Cold Ash added to Hampton Court & Kew Gardens, Sandbanks, Corfe Castle, Swanage & Lulworth Cove, Hurst Park, Kempton Park, Sandown Park, Twickenham Rugby. New coastal express from Cold Ash to Brighton via Thatcham – Newbury – Winchester – Bognor Regis – littlehampton – Worthing.

25.6.55 – New express carriage from Newbury Camp Close to Thatcham Depot via Shaw, Thatcham – Midgham – Brimpton – Aldermaston AWRE. Additional contract to AWRE starting from Wash Common. New express carriage from Baydon to AWRE Aldermaston via Lambourn Woodlands – Shefford Woodlands – Wickham – Stockcross – Speen – Newbury – Thatcham.

29.10.55 – New express carriage from Newbury to Associated Electrical Industries (Aldermaston Court) via Thatcham and Woolhampton.

24.12.55 – New coastal express carriage from Cold Ash to Weymouth via Thatcham – Newbury – Winchester – Bournemouth – Wareham and Wool – **refused, and lost on appeal.**

21.1.56 – New express carriage from Hampstead Norris to Harwell AERE via Aldworth and West Ilsley.

New express carriage from Lilley to RAF Welford via Brightwalton – Chaddleworth – Lambourn – Eastbury – East Garston – Shefford – Weston -Welford Village. Also to RAF Welford from Newbury (Hambridge Road) via Newbury – Speen – Boxford – Leckhampstead – Thicket.

14.9.57 – New express carriage to AERE Harwell from Newbury, via Donnington – Chieveley – Beedon.

*1.2.58 – E&Ts from Thatcham via Newbury additions A Blackpool 3-day tour, Eire via Holyhead 7/8-day tour – **Thames Valley objected on behalf of South Midland, so refused and appeal was lost***

3.58 – New express carriage Newbury to Milton (RAF Unit), via Chieveley – Langley Hall – Chaddleworth – Brightwalton – Farnborough – West Ilsley. 3 New express carriages to Vickers Armstrong Aircraft Factory at South Marston from Newbury via Sotockcross – Wickham - Shefford Woodlands – Lambourn Woodlands – Baydon, plus from Shaw via Newbury – Wash Water – Wash Common – Valley Road – Enborne Road, and from Newtown Common via Newbury. Additional feeder service to AWRE Aldermaston as Kintbury – Inkpen Common – Hungerford. Also feeder from Hermitage to Baydon to meet existing contract journeys for AERE Harwell.

30.5.57 - Taken over from Sis Taylor (Enterprise), Newbury – (business absorbed 1/65) Express carriage from London (Baylis Road Coach Park) to USAAF Base, Greenham Common via Slough and Reading.

18.7.59 – Additions to E&Ts from each of Cold Ash, Brightwalton and Yattendon to Royal Agricultural Show, Bath & West Show, Royal Counties Show.

11.4.59 – New express carriages to Didcot (Central Ordnance Depot) from Newbury via Chieveley – Downend – Beedon – East Ilsley – West Ilsley – Didcot, and from Kintbury via Weston – Great Shefford – East Garston – Eastbury – Lambourn – Didcot, and from Newbury via Hermitage – Hampstead Norris – Compton – East Ilsley – Chilton – Didcot.

3.12.60 -Additions to E&Ts from Newbury via Thatcham and Yattendon to 29 destinations for away fixtures of Newbury FC. Also additional local pick-up points added to long list of existing 58 E&Ts. A lot of the existing contracts to AERE Harwell also re-organised at that point, with some Harwell contract numbers actually quoted. Also confirmed route of

Aldbourne to AWRE Alderrmaston as via Ramsbury – Witton Ditch – Chilton Foliat – Hungerford – Kintbury Station – Halfway.

6.5.61- During renewals of E&Ts from Newbury etc.the following added as M1 Motorway Tour, Gatwick Airport, Lockinge (Point to Point), Wisley Gardens, Slimbridge Wildfowl Trust and New Cross (Stock Car Racing).

12.1.63 – Re-organisation of routes to Vickers-Armstrong Factory at South Marston, now starting from Newtown, Burghclere and Thatcham.

30.11.63 – Additional E&Ts from Yattendon via Thatcham and Newbury to Frensham Ponds, Guildford Cathedral, London (Crystal Palace), Southend-on-Sea, London Tour, Circular tours via Abingdon & Wantage and Hungerford & Winchester. Also new express carriage to AERE Harwell from Lambourn via Baydon, and from Hungerford via Chilton Foliat – Lambourn Woodlands – Shefford Woodlands – Shefford – in part due to new working hours at AERE and a general re-casting of its own direct transport operations.

30.5.64 – Additional E&Ts added as Bristol Zoo & Clifton, Berkeley Castle, Milford-on-Sea. Brighton express upgraded with additional local pick-ups.

30.5.64- To take over license from Thames Valley as Newbury to Fairmile Hospital via Midgham – Woolhampton Thatcham and Pangbourne- started by Durnford Bros. in the 1930's.

9.1.65 – New express carriages to Hungerford (Chilton Electrics) from Sold Ash via Thatcham – Newbury – Speen – Elcot – Kintbury and from Newbury via Valley Road – Emborne and Kintbury

2.10.65 – New express carriage to AERE Harwell from Bucklebury via Thatcham – Henwick – Shaw – Hermitage – Hampstead Norris.

8.1.66 – Licences not renewed for London (Baylis Road CP) to USAAF Greenham Common and to RAF Abingdon (both former Enterprise Contracts).

5.3.66 – New express carriage to AERE Harwell from Frilsham via Yattendon – Hampstead Norris – Compton – East Ilsley.

28.5.66 - Additional E&Ts from Thatcham via Newbury to Lee-on-Solent, Longleat House, Whipsnade Zoo, Wooburn Abbey, London Zoo,

Epsom, Goodwood Races, Farnborough Air Show, Wye Valley Tour.

12.11.66 – Additional E&Ts to Barry Island, Gosport, Beaulieu, Windsor & Saville Garden.

9.7.66 – License surrendered as Stage Carriage from Newbury to Wantage.

7.1.67 – Licenses not renewed to Armstrong Vickers Factory at South Marston and from Newbury to Didcot (Central Ordnance Depot)

14.10.67 – Additional tour license 3-day tour to Northern France via Dover.

6.1.68 – License not renewed express carriages to Hungerford (Chilton Electrics).

2.3.68 – Licenses surrendered for Stage Carriage Newbury to Cold Ash and Newbury to Brightwalton.

25.10.69 – Additional E&Ts to The Brecon Beacons, Syon House, Windsor Safari Park. Also, generally increased pick-ups on E&Ts to include Headley and Kingsclere, as well as RAF Station Greenham Common.

12.1.71 Express carriages altered to run as Wantage to Greenham Common and to Welford (RAF Station).

9.2.74 – Not renewed express carriage Newbury to RAF Welford.

27.12.75 – Not renewed Hungerford to AERE Harwell.

23.7.77 – Donnington to AWRE Aldermaston approved for double-deck working.

Another nice line up of Reliance coaches shows No.90 (OLU 527) with the oval style of Duple 'Super Vega' grille, then No.74 (YMO 524), with later style, then No.83 (TEL 700), an 'AEC Reliance' with unusual Plaxton 'Consort' body, formerly in the high-class touring fleet of Excelsior Coaches of Bournemouth.

However, it was the fate of a few of the vehicles over the years to 'retire to the orchard' where parts were removed, so here we see (above) the once pride-of-the-fleet Vincent-bodied AEC 'Regal' No. 21 (EJB 584), whilst (below) the Thurgood-bodied Bedford OB No.37 (KKX 40) in advanced 'naturalisation'!

APPENDIX 2 - RELIANCE MOTOR SERVICES FLEET LIST 1922 - 1986

Fleet No	Reg. No.	Chassis Make & Type	Bodybuilder	Layout	Date New	Date In	Date Out
None	BL 8886	Ford Model T	Andrews	Van14	Jun-22	New	Dec-29
None	MO 3314	Ford Model T Tonbus	Andrews	B14	Aug-24	New	Oct-30
None	??	Talbot 25/50hp	Andrews	C14D	??	??/25	??
None	RX 4556	Ford AA	Andrews?	C14D	May-29	New	Sep-32
4	VD 488	Gilford 168OT	Wycombe	C32F	Mar-31	Dec-34	Jan-45
5	RX 8373	Dodge B-type	Wilmott	B14F	Apr-31	Jun-34	Dec-36
None	RX 6888	Ford AA	Duple	C14D	Jun-30	New	Sep-32
1	RX 8261	Ford AA	Andrews	B20F	Mar-31	Dec-34	May-38
2 (10)	MY 3462	Gilford 168SD	Duple (later Heaver)	C26F	Mar-30	Dec-34	Oct-49
3	SH 3380	GMC T30C	Alexander	B20F	May-29	Dec-34	Dec-36
None	RX 8171	Ford AA	??	C18D	Feb-31	??/35	May-38
7	AKE 393	Commer Centaur	Duple	C20F	Dec-32	??/38	??
8	GL 2386	Commer Centaur	Duple	C20F	??/35	??/37	???45
9	JB 4789	Bedford WLB	Duple	C20F	Oct-34	Jun-38	Dec-40
11	DY 9486	Commer PNF4	Harrington	FC24F	Apr-36	Dec-40	Aug-51
18	VH 4682	AEC Regal 662	NCME	B32R	??/33	Dec-52	Apr-57
10	MW 2985	GMC T19	Heaver (Re-body)	C???	Oct-28	Jan-41	Dec-53
12	CMO 600	Bedford OWB	Duple	UB32F	Jan-43	New	Sep-57
13	UF 8832	Leyland Tiger TS4	Lambourn Garage	C33F	Jun-32	??/43	Mar-60
14	CRX 34	Bedford OWB	Duple	UB32F	Jan-44	New	Dec-52
15	CRX 682	Bedford OWB	Duple MkII	B30F	Oct-45	New	Apr-58
16	DJB 406	Bedford OB	Duple Vista	C29F	Oct-46	New	Jun-57
19	EBL 430	Bedford OB	Duple Vista	C29F	Oct-47	New	Sep-65
20	FPT 313	Bedford OWB	SMT	UB30F	Dec-43	Mar-48	Aug-55
21	EJB 584	AEC Regal 0662	Vincent	C33F	Apr-48	New	Mar-61
17	WN8978	Dennis Lancet MkII	Weymann	B32F	Nov-36	Jun-48	Nov-54
23	ERX 284	Bedford OB	Duple Vista	C29F	Dec-48	New	Oct-68
24	FMO 145	Commer Avenger 23A	Strachan	C33F	Feb-50	New	Feb-55
22	RX 6250	Leyland Tiger TS3	Brush	B29R	Jun-30	Jul-50	Not run
25	ABL 760	Leyland Tiger TS7	ECW	B35R	Mar-37	Sep-50	Apr-57
26	GJB 491	Bedford SB	Duple Vega	C33F	??/51	New	Nov-63
27	JB 7499	Leyland Tiger TS7	Brush	B35R	Dec-35	Feb-51	Jul-55
31	GYB 625	Bedford OWB	Duple MkII	B30F	Nov-45	Jun-51	Nov-63
29	NRE 234	Bedford OB	Duple Vista	C29F	Apr-47	Apr-52	Dec-59
28	HON 623	AEC Regal 9621A	Burlingham	C33F	Sep-48	Jun-52	Aug-64
30	HRX 10	Bedford SB	B'ham Baby Seagull	C35F	May-53	New	Jan-67
33	EFC 285	AEC Regal 0662	Weymann	B34F	Apr-37	May-53	Apr-55
32	EFC 286	AEC Regal 0662	Weymann	B34F	Apr-37	May-53	Apr-59
34	JRX 867	AEC Reliance MU3RV	Burlingham Seagull	C41C	May-54	New	May-71
35	ABL 757	Leyland Tiger TS7	ECW	B35R	Mar-37	??/55	??/??
36	LBL 197	AEC Reliance MU3RV	Burlingham Seagull	C41C	May-55	New	Apr-71
37	KKX40	Bedford OB	Thurgood	C29F	Jul-47	May-55	By 3/61
38	HOB 941	Bedford OB	Duple Vista	C29F	May-47	May-55	Nov-62
39	DLU 92	AEC Regent 0661	LPTB	H56R	May-37	Aug-55	May-58
40	DGX 206	AEC Regent 0661	LPTB	H56R	??/36	Oct-55	May-58
41	DDL 924	Bedford OB	Duple MkII	B29F	Jan-46	Nov-55	Dec-59
42	ETM 649	Guy Arab MkIII 5LW	Thurgood	C35F	??/46	Nov-55	Sep-60
43	ETM 650	Guy Arab MkIII 5LW	Thurgood	C35F	??/46	Nov-55	Sep-60
44	DKT 25	AEC Regal 0662	Harrington	B34F	Jun-37	Jun-56	Nov-59
45	DKT 18	AEC Regal 0662	Harrington	B34F	Jun-37	Mar-56	Dec-57
46	MJB 820	AEC Reliance MU3RV	Burlingham Seagull	C41C	May-56	New	Feb-73
47	ABE 957	AEC Regal 0662	Barnaby	DP32F	Jun-38	May-56	Apr-62
48	TMY 941	Bedford OB	Duple Vista	C29F	??/49	Sep-56	Mar-61
49	HYF 971	Bedford OB	Duple Vista	C25F	Apr-47	Sep-56	Dec-63
50	CVT 684	AEC Regal MkII 0862	Duple	B39F	Mar-36	Jan-57	Dec-59
None	JO 5035	AEC Regal 4 642	Harrington	C33F	Jul-32	By 3/57	Not run
51	CN 9547	AEC Regent 0661	Weymann	H56R	May-40	Mar-57	Dec-60

Fleet No	Reg. No.	Chassis Make & Type	Bodybuilder	Layout	Date New	Date In	Date Out
52	JVK 633	AEC Regent MkI 0661	Weymann	H56R	Mar-46	Dec-57	Jul-62
53	CWV 430	Bedford OWB	Lee (Re-bodied)	C29F	Jul-42	Dec-57	May-64
54	HYP 722	Bedford OB	Duple Vista	C29F	Feb-48	Dec-57	May-65
55	FGB 184	AEC Regal MkIII 0962	Duple A-type	C33F	Jul-47	Dec-57	Feb-63
56	EWV 396	AEC Regal MkIII 0962	Duple A-type	C33F	Nov-47	Dec-57	Jun-66
57	BUS 168	AEC Regent MkI 0661	Scottish Aviation	H56R	Jun-38	Dec-57	Dec-62
60	SME 84	AEC Regal 0662	Duple (1954)	FC35F	Jul-47	Dec-58	Oct-65
58	HWJ 991	AEC Regal 0662	Duple A-type	C35F	Sep-49	Jan-59	Nov-62
61	OMX 325	AEC Regal Mk111 9621A	Duple A-type	C33F	Mar-50	Jan-59	May-64
62	BGA 9	AEC Regent 0661	Coweison	H56R	Sep-37	Feb-59	May-64
59	CRP 300	AEC Regal 0662	Duple (1955)	C35F	Jun-46	Mar-59	Oct-61
None	BGA 6	AEC Regent 0661	Coweison	H56R	Sep-37	Mar-59	Not run
66	BGA 19	AEC Regent 0661	Alexander	H56R	Oct-37	Mar-59	Feb-65
63	LPA 952	AEC Regal 0662	Harrington	C33F	Jun-47	Oct-59	Nov-63
64	LPA 951	AEC Regal 0662	Harrington	C33F	May-47	Nov-59	Aug-61
65	JTX 667	AEC Regal Mk111 9621E	Burlingham	C33F	??/50	Feb-60	Jun-64
67	VMO 440	AEC Reliance 2MU3RV	Duple Britannia	C41C	Jul-60	New	Jul-75
68	PAD 587	AEC Reliance MU3RV	Duple Elizabethan	C41C	May-55	Sep-60	Jun-71
69	LUY 750	AEC Regal 0662	Yeates (1953)	C38F	Mar-38	Dec-60	Jun-64
70	208 BRE	Bedford SBO	Duple	C36F	??/54	Dec-60	Oct-65
71	219 BRE	Bedford SBO	Duple Super Vega	C36F	??/54	Dec-60	Jul-65
72	329 ABJ	Austin J2VA	Kenex	B11F	??/58	Apr-61	Jun-69
73	NTH 690	Bedford SBO	Duple Midland	B40F	Dec-56	Sep-61	Aug-66
74	YMO 324	Bedford SB1	Duple Super Vega	C41F	Aug-61	New	Oct-75
75	NUY 331	Bedford SBO	Duple Midland	B40F	Oct-54	Aug-61	Mar-67
77	AEY 175	Bedford SB	Plaxton	C36F	Apr-52	Oct-61	Nov-65
76	OLD 142	Bedford SBO	Harrington	C36F	Feb-54	Jan-62	Jan-67
78	DCK 219	Leyland Titan PD2/3	East Lancs	FL49RD	Jan-51	Oct-62	Nov-66
79	453 BMO	Bedford SB5	Duple Super Vega	C41F	Jul-62	New	Jul-75
80	SX 8901	Bedford SBO	Duple Midland	B40F	??/54	Nov-62	Jun-66
82	SX 8902	Bedford SBO	Duple Midland	B40F	??/54	Nov-62	Jun-66
81	HXB 457	AEC Regal 0662	Duple A-type	C35F	Aug-46	Dec-62	Nov-67
83	TEL 700	AEC Reliance MU3RA	Plaxton Consort	C41C	??/56	Feb-63	May-71
84	LVA 271	AEC Reliance MU3RV	PlaxtonVenturer II	C41C	Apr-55	Feb-63	May-68
85	MWL 972	AEC Regent MkII 0661	Weymann	H56RD	Jul-48	May-63	Oct-68
86	MWL 978	AEC Regent MkII 0661	Weymann	H56RD	Jul-48	Jun-63	Oct-68
87	504 EBL	Bedford VAL14	Vega Major	C52F	Jun-63	New	Oct-84
88	OGT 310	Bedford SBG	Duple Super Vega	C34F	??/54	Aug-63	Jan-67
90	OLU 527	Bedford SBG	Duple Super Vega	C34F	??/54	Aug-63	Feb-67
89	SKR 443	Bedford SBG	PlaxtonVenturer II	C38F	May-54	Sep-63	Feb-67
91	MAW 44	Bedford SBO	Duple Super Vega	C38F	Mar-55	Oct-63	Jan-67
92	OEL 931	Bedford SBO	Duple Super Vega	C38F	Mar-54	Nov-63	Jun-65
93	OEL 932	Bedford SBO	Duple Super Vega	C38F	Apr-54	Nov-63	Dec-64
94	OEL 933	Bedford SBO	Duple Super Vega	C38F	Apr-54	Nov-63	Dec-65
95	OEL 935	Bedford SBO	Duple Super Vega	C38F	Apr-54	Nov-63	Jun-64
96	KNV 442	AEC Reliance MU3RV	Duple Elizabethan	C41C	??/54	May-64	May-71
97	MHO 363	AEC Reliance MU3RV	Mann Egerton	C43F	May-54	??/64	Jun-69
None	234 AMY	Bedford SBG	Duple Super Vega	C38F	??/??	Jun-64	Jun-65
98	BBL 665B	Bedford SB13	Duple (N) Firefly	C41F	Jul-64	New	May-77
99	ULJ 800	AEC Reliance MU3RA	Plaxton Consort	C41C	??/57	Oct-64	Oct-72
100	939 ARP	Morris J2BM	BMC	B11F	??/62	Dec-64	Jul-66
101	775 CD	Morris J2BM	BMC	B11F	??/62	Dec-64	Jul-66
102	796 BOR	Morris J2BM	BMC	B11F	Apr-61	Dec-64	Jul-66
103	DRX 747C	Bedford SB5	Duple Bella Vega	C41F	Jun-65	New	Oct-78
104	DRX 748C	Bedford SB5	Duple Bella Vega	C41F	Jun-65	New	Jan-81
105	REL 55	Bedford SB8	Duple Super Vega	C38F	Mar-55	Feb-65	Nov-66
106	REL 57	Bedford SB8	Duple Super Vega	C38F	Mar-55	Feb-65	Nov-66
107	REL 54	Bedford SB8	Duple Super Vega	C38F	Mar-55	Feb-65	Nov-66

Fleet No	Reg. No.	Chassis Make & Type	Bodybuilder	Layout	Date New	Date In	Date Out
108	XBK 40	Bedford SB1	Duple Super Vega	C41F	Mar-61	Sep-65	Sep-74
109	KCP 725	Bedford SB3	Plaxton Consort	C41F	Jan-59	Mar-66	Nov-72
110	GRX 398D	Bedford VAM5	Duple Bella Venture	C45F	Mar-66	New	Sep-80
111	GRX 399D	Bedford VAM5	Duple Bella Venture	C45F	Mar-66	New	Sep-80
112	289 FNK	Bedford SB3	Duple Super Vega	C41F	Jan-59	Nov-66	Sep-74
113	WLB 420	Bedford SB3	Duple Super Vega	C41F	Apr-59	Nov-66	Sep-74
114	4590 WA	Bedford SB3	Duple Super Vega	C41F	Mar-60	Nov-66	Feb-73
116	XOU 377	Bedford SB1	Pton Consort MkIV	C41F	May-60	Jan-67	Sep-74
115	6706 WE	Bedford SB3	Pton Consort MkIV	C41F	Mar-59	Jan-67	Nov-72
120	CBL 488B	Morris J2VM16	Deansgate	B12	??/64	Feb-67	??
117	AMC 351A	Bedford SB8	Pton Embassy MkII	C41F	May-63	Mar-67	Mar-78
118	AMC 352A	Bedford SB8	Pton Embassy MkII	C41F	May-63	Sep-67	Oct-75
119	200 GMY	AEC Reliance MU3RV	Duple Britannia	C30F	??/58	Sep-67	Mar-71
124	5900 EL	Bedford SB1	Harrington Crusader	C41F	May-60	Jan-68	May-72
None	7402 EL	Bedford SB1	Harrington Crusader	C41F	Jul-60	Jan-68	Not run
None	7403EL	Bedford SB1	Harrington Crusader	C41F	Jul-60	Jan-68	Not run
123	7467 FH	Commer 1500LBD	Harrington	B12	Jan-63	Feb-68	Aug-74
122	600 DBU	Bedford SB5	Pton Embassy MkII	C41F	Apr-63	May-68	Jul-78
121	KMD 440C	Bedford SB5	Duple Bella Vega	C41F	??/65	Jun-68	Mar-81
125	ROD 767	AEC Regent MkV	MCCW	H59RD	Jul-56	Aug-68	Dec-77
126	TTT 781	AEC Regent MkV	MCCW	H59RD	Jun-59	Aug-68	Dec-77
128	RHK 701D	Bedford SB5	Duple Bella Vega	C41F	Jun-66	Apr-69	Nov-78
127	VBL 413G	Ford R226	Pton Panorama Elite	C52F	Jun-69	New	May-82
129	URO 915E	Bedford VAM5	Plaxton Panorama	C45F	Jul-67	Sep-69	Feb-79
130	URX 238H	Ford Transit	Ford	B12	Sep-69	New	May-76
131	XMO 455H	Ford R226	Pton Panorama Elite	C52F	May-70	New	May-82
132	FGF 474C	Bedford SB13	Duple Bella Vega	C41F	Jun-65	Feb-71	Aug-76
134	CWH 788C	Bedford SB13	Plaxton Panorama	C41F	Jan-65	Mar-71	Aug-76
135	EAD 361C	Bedford SB5	Duple Bella Vega	C41F	May-65	Mar-71	Apr-78
136	DJH 733F	Bedford VAM70	Duple Viceroy	C45F	Jun-68	Apr-71	Sep-80
133	BSY 418C	Bedford SB5	Duple Bella Vega	C41F	Oct-65	May-71	Sep-78
138	ODD 166F	Bedford SB5	Plaxton Panorama	C41F	Jun-68	Oct-72	Aug-82
139	FUP 572H	Bedford SB5	Pton Panorama II	C41F	Mar-69	Nov-72	Jul-82
140	DJH 750G	Bedford VAM70	PlaxtonElite	C45F	Mar-69	Nov-72	Jul-82
137	JRL 552E	Bedford VAM14	Pton Panorama II	C45F	Jun-67	Feb-73	Feb-79
144	ULT 442M	Ford Transit	Bristol Street	B12	May-74	New	Jun-85
141	UJB 725N	Bedford YRQ	Duple Dominant	C45F	Aug-74	New	Nov-84
142	UJB 726N	Bedford YRQ	Duple Dominant	C45F	Aug-74	New	Nov-84
143	UJB 727N	Bedford YRQ	Duple Dominant	C53F	Aug-74	New	Dec-85
145	HGM 820M	Bedford SB5	Duple Dominant	C41F	Jul-75	New	Dec-82
147	HGM 822N	Bedford YRQ	Duple Dominant	C45F	Jun-75	New	Dec-85
146	KCF 27P	Bedford SB5	Duple Dominant	C41F	Oct-75	New	Oct-83
151	NJM7P	Ford Transit	Tricentrol	B12	May-76	New	Oct-84
149	LTF 224P	Bedford YMT	Duple Dominant	C53F	Jun-76	New	Dec-85
150	NMO 66R	Bedford YMT	Duple Dominant	C53F	Jan-77	New	New
148	EDW 420L	Ford Transit (non PSV)	Ford	B12	??/72	Jan-77	??/??
152	OAN 962R	Bedford YLQ	Duple Dominant	C45F	May-77	New	Dec-85
153	OAN 963R	Bedford YLQ	Duple Dominant	C45F	May-77	New	Dec-85
154	OAN 964R	Bedford YLQ	Duple Dominant	C45F	May-77	New	Dec-85
155	.TWR 771M	Bedford YRQ	Plaxton Elite	C45F	Jun-74	Sep-77	Jul-85
156	TOT 245M	Bedford YRQ	Duple Dominant	C45F	Jun-74	Apr-78	Dec-85
157	KPC 213P	Bedford YRQ	Duple Dominant	C45F	Sep-75	Apr-78	Dec-85
159	LDN 513N	Bedford YRT	Pton Supreme	C53F	Jun-75	Nov-78	Aug-85
158	TWR 772M	Bedford YRQ	Plaxton Elite	C45F	Jun-74	Nov-78	Aug-85
160	YCF 966T	Ford R1114	Duple Dominant II	C53F	May-79	New	Aug-85
161	YCF 967T	Ford R1114	Duple Dominant II	C53F	May-79	New	Aug-85
162	ERX 251V	Ford R1114	Pton Supreme III	C53F	May-80	New	Dec-85
163	ERX 252V	Ford R1114	Pton Supreme III	C53F	May-80	New	Jan-86

95

Fleet No	Reg. No.	Chassis Make & Type	Bodybuilder	Layout	Date New	Date In	Date Out
164	NWD 779P	Ford R1114	Pton Supreme	C49F	Jul-67	Apr-81	Jan-84
165	KBL 251W	Bedford YNT	Duple Dominant III	C53F	Apr-81	New	!2/85
166	KBL 252W	Bedford YNT	Duple Dominant III	C53F	Apr-81	New	!2/85
167	DEV 217T	Ford Escort	NPSV Van	N/A	Apr-81	New	Dec-85
168	BPG 777T	Bedford YMT	Pton Supreme IV	C53F	Mar-79	May-82	Dec-85
169	YPB 837T	Bedford YMT	Pton Supreme IV	C53F	Jan-79	May-82	Dec-85
170	LVS 435V	Bedford YMT	Pton Supreme IV	C53F	Apr-80	May-82	Dec-85
171	TJH 883Y	Mercedes Benz 0309	Devon Conversions	C19F	Apr-83	New	Dec-85
172	TJH 882Y	Bedford YNT	Pton Paramount	C53F	Apr-83	New	Dec-85
173	TJH 881Y	Bedford YNT	Pton Paramount	C53F	Apr-83	New	Dec-85
174	FKX 275T	Bedford YMT	Duple Dominant II	C53F	Apr-79	Dec-83	Dec-85
175	A64YRD	FIAT 35.B	Robin Hood	C12	Mar-84	New	Dec-85
176	VPR 864X	Bedford YNT	Pton Supreme IV	C53F	Oct-81	Aug-84	Dec-85
177	FYD 523Y	Bedford YNT	Duple Dominant IV	C53F	Sep-82	Oct-84	Jan-86
178	FYD 524Y	Bedford YNT	Duple Dominant IV	C53F	Sep-82	Oct-84	Dec-85

The end of Reliance Stage Carriage Operations - 24th June 1966.

With over-riding concerns over possible Nationalisation or absorbtion into a PTE, the Reliance Directors took the decision to discontinue the stage carriage operations in the Summer of 1966, having first contacted Thames Valley to ensure some continuity of provision. Both the Cold Ash and Brightwalton routes were turning a profit, so Cold Ash became the 107 and Brightwalton the 119 from 25th June 1966, but the loss-making Wantage was not continued by TV.

The mainstay of the bus operations for many years were the Bedford SBO's with Duple Midland bodies, 2 of which are shown on the final day of operations, both 1954 examples in this photo by Philip Wallis.
80 (SX 8901) was driven by Alan Coxhead with conductress Jean Bailey for Cold Ash at 18.00, whilst 75 (NUY 331) was driven by Harry Talbot and left for Brightwalton ast 18.15.